MAN...
F@#K!

THE
HONEST
REALITY of
ENTREPRENEURSHIP

ROD F. MARCHAND

Published by Mindstir Media, LLC
45 Lafayette Rd | Suite 181| North Hampton, NH 03862 | USA
1.800.767.0531 | www.mindstirmedia.com

Printed in the United States of America
ISBN-13: 978-1-7352710-7-1

TABLE OF CONTENTS

Dedication v

Man...F@#K! Foreword vii

Introduction 1

The Beginning 5

Little Rod's Growing Up 9

Living the Dream 14

The Wakeup Call 22

The Prodigal Son Returns 26

New Beginnings 30

It Was the Best of Times, It Was the
Worst of Times 33

Mentorship, Friendship and Companionship...
Oh My! 37

Lighting Strikes 43

Reconciliation 47

The Hits Keep Coming 53

There's a Light at the End of the Tunnel...
I Hope it's Not a Train! 57

Don't Get Me Wrong... We Like Trains! 61

I Went For a Drive 69

If You Can't Beat Them, Join Them! 77

By the Power of the Holy Spirit 84

Mi Familia 93

We Won't Be Fooled Again... 99

Failure to Launch 105

The Call 109

The Dynamic DUO 117

The Waiting is the Hardest Part! 122

That Was Easy... Not! 127

Sweet Home Chicago 133

Return of the Jedi 137

COVID 19 – The Man...F@#k! Heard
Around the World! 143

Schadenfreude! 146

Going From "Really Good" to "Great" 151

Acknowledgements 155

About the Author 157

DEDICATION

I would like to dedicate this book to my wife Angie. We have been through so much together and I know that this book wouldn't be possible without you! You always believed in what we could achieve together, even when you shouldn't have! You have always been the one who has kept our family together during times of struggle and you have been my anchor when I was adrift! When everything seemed lost, there you were keeping my ego in check, while still giving me the confidence to press on. You have been an outstanding mother and business partner through all of it, and you have been the glue holding it all together. I can't express the gratitude, love and support I have for you, and all the love you have given. I want to thank you for believing in me and our vision together!

I would also like to dedicate this book to my children. We have been through so much together. You always supported me and understood the late nights and the work required to get the job done. I know that at times you thought of me as your Superman, but I didn't always meet up to the challenge! I hope you know how much I love each and every one of you. You were always the catalyst to drive forward for something better. The commitment of Quincy and Spencer, who have now joined us in the family business can't be expressed with enough gratitude. You could do anything in life, yet chose to take a chance on your father's dreams!

Finally, my parents. Thank you for guiding me and teaching me all the needed aspects of what it takes to run a family business. My start couldn't have come from anything more than your belief in me and the risk you took allowing me to try. Growing up in a family business has taught me so much, and everything I know about integrity, finance, humility, values and hard work have come from you first and foremost. I am so proud of what you started and what we have been able to build upon ever since.

MAN...F@#K! FOREWORD

by **Kevin Harrington**,

Original Shark from ABC's Hit TV Show "Shark Tank" and Inventor of the Infomercial;

Renowned Public Speaker and Bestselling Author of *Act Now; How I Turn Ideas into Million-Dollar Products, Key Person of Influence, and Put a Shark in Your Tank*

As a pioneer of the *As Seen On TV* industry responsible for over $5 billion in product sales, I've worked with hundreds of business owners over the years. The strongest qualities that set entrepreneurs apart are *ambition* and *fearlessness*. When Rod Marchand and I met at my pitch event in 2019, it was apparent that once he set his mind to building a successful business, there was no stopping him. It was my pleasure to endorse Accord Comfort Sleep Systems, and I was honored to write this foreword for the publishing of his first book.

One of the most common mistakes I see entrepreneurs make is overthinking their ideas instead of acting. While most people are second-guessing their decisions and letting doubt hold them back, true entrepreneurs are *doing*. Rod Marchand has always been one of those people. He spent his life turning a solid family furniture business into a budding empire. From developing innovative new mattress products to wearing every hat in the company, Rod's scrappy business mentality has been the secret to his success. He has never been afraid of stepping out of his comfort zone to help his company evolve and grow.

Man...F@#K! is a down-to-earth account of an everyday man's journey in entrepreneurship. It is a personal and professional peek inside the life of a business owner, husband and father of 7. In this first book published by Rod Marchand, readers can experience the rollercoaster of starting and running a business, with all the accompanying highs and lows. Rod teaches us that no matter how many times you stop and say "man...f@#k!" you shake it off and keep pushing forward.

As a lifelong entrepreneur, I myself have experienced the same adventures continuously throughout the years. Reading Rod's story took me back to some of my own memories and lessons learned...all leading to where I am today. The journey is not over for either of us, and hopefully Rod's stories will help other entrepreneurs realize they're not alone. Keep pushing, with ambition and fearlessness...and most of all, a positive mindset! Enjoy the book...

Signed,
Kevin Harrington

INTRODUCTION

Let me start by saying that I am not an advocate for foul language, although I am also not a Boy Scout! My choice of book title was to convey those moments in life, whether it be in business or day to day, where we find ourselves face with this familiar sentiment Man F@#k!

I also have to admit that this is not my original idea. I was at a comedy club at the Atlantis Resort in February of 1999. I happened to be on vacation with one of my longtime friends and then-employee who had a connection with management at the resort to arrange complimentary accommodation. Technically, I should never have been staying at that resort at that time, but we'll talk more about the reasons for my stay and the circumstances surrounding it later in the book. At the time I was feeling high levels of anxiety and frustration, so a comedy show seemed to be a welcomed distraction! The opening act came out, introduced himself, and proceeded to tell us that he was working on a book. He paused and remarked that he was thinking the title might be... Man...F@#k! I nearly spat my drink out onto my friends. I related to the title as if it were a book about my very life! Unfortunately, I can't remember the comedian's name in order to give him the credit, but the title and idea have stuck with me ever since. To whoever you are, and wherever you are, thank you!

The purpose of this book is to help all entrepreneurs, business owners, or simply individuals who are thinking about taking on a new job or business venture. I am here to acknowledge all the challenges and risks that you will likely encounter, but also to encourage you with all the possible rewards for taking a chance on yourself. We all know life is full of ups and downs, but when you have skin in the game, the downs can seem extremely overwhelming. I want to encourage you to dream big and believe in yourself. Our company had a humble start in a community with a population of just 2,000 people. It has now grown into a potentially global company and brand. Don't fall into the trap of the *'who am I'* or *'I can't do this'* mentality or way of thinking; if you believe it, you can achieve it! Not that it doesn't take a tremendous amount of effort and commitment, but anything is possible if you have the right attitude and surround yourself with the right people. From humble beginnings to future success, the journey may be tough but it's not impossible!

I want to take this time to thank everyone who has inspired me along the way and supported me in my business and ideas, especially my wife Angie, my children, my parents, my staff and so many of our customers and business partners that have helped me along the way. I truly love you all! The main person responsible for getting this book written was Kevin Harrington, the 'Original Shark from Shark Tank'. I was able to personally meet Kevin at one of his many events called the *Innovator's Think Tank*. I'll talk more about this experience later in the book, but something that really stuck with me was what he said at the end of a talk he gave. He mentioned the power of reading and being inspired by innovative, motivational books. Then he asked the question: "Has anyone here published a book? If so, I would love to read it!" That was all it took. I had writing this book on my list of goals for years, but never seemed to find the time to get started. I would simply just pass it along, year after year, and hope to one day find the time. Then I remembered someone saying to me, "We all have the same twenty-four hours in a day. Your success is determined by how well you use them." And you know what? It really is the truth! This is simply my story, not an instruction manual, although I do hope that you can glean some good things from it and put them into practice. Now, let's get started.

THE BEGINNING

My love for business and entrepreneurship started at a very young age. My father retired from the Navy in 1980 and decided to move us from beautiful Honolulu, Hawaii, to beautiful Harvey, North Dakota. As you can probably guess, even at the age of eight, this was my first Man...F@#k! moment! I still give my father a hard time about this decision all these years later. He was my first inside look at what an entrepreneur was all about, as through him I was learning the inner workings of our trade, designing logos, stationery, and of course, what to call this new business and how to make an impact. Don't get me wrong, he wasn't seeking business advice from an eight-year old, but it was his way of bonding with me and instilling an early love for building things. Most of this work can go on for years before your dream becomes a reality. It takes an abundance of creative planning, and the more people involved, the less everyone agrees! This is usually the very first lesson in entrepreneurship and leadership. Learning to collaborate and find the best possible plan of execution - even if not everyone agrees, - is a practice my kids can also testify to, as most of them have been active in our second-generation expansions throughout the years. We'll get into more about my family later, but for now let's stay focused on the beginning.

Once my parents had opened the business, like any mom-and-pop store, I spent most of my time after school and on weekends there.

I was excited about the business and enjoyed the industry. We were an electronics dealer and repair shop, and I enjoyed learning about the trade. I spent many hours with my father in the repair shop learning all the intricate details of the field of electronics, specifically how to troubleshoot television and radio issues. I listened to my mother on the showroom floor, selling new products to customers, and learned the importance of how to communicate with a customer and build rapport and lasting relationships. I am happy to say that even as I write this, my office is in the very same showroom as our original location, which consisted of a whopping five televisions and two home stereos! We are no longer in that industry, but it was here that my love for business began.

I was so excited after our first year in business that for the next school year, I was allowed to pick out my own attire from the JC Penney's catalog. I knew instantly that there would be no more jeans and T-shirts for me; I chose the slacks and polo shirts, with matching belt to be sure. I was going to be a business professional, and certainly needed to look the part. The only thing missing was a briefcase. I asked my parents if I could buy one, but like most startup companies, money was tight, and the answer was no. Even at a young age, however, it was evident that I thought outside the box, and I noticed a backgammon game that nobody played with anymore. I simply emptied the contents, and although it was a little small, I filled it with a calculator, pens, paper and some business cards and... voila, a briefcase! I know you're probably thinking, '*What a nerd!*', but I like to think that I was a pretty cool nerd. I certainly had chutzpah. I used to talk about work and business to all my friends, which of course they loved (because what eight-year old kid doesn't love business?!) and even tried to sell them and their parents the latest electronics. I am proud to say I was able to do that on a couple of occasions, and the passion for sales was already becoming a very big part of who I was.

As I mentioned earlier, I spent a lot of time at the shop with my parents, and so when there were times that I couldn't be of any help, my dad let me set up my own work shop/office space in the basement of the store. I also had a love of chemistry and was able to save enough money while working to purchase my very first chemistry set. I had an electronics shop, chemistry lab and corporate office of my very own, at the neat young age of ten. I even created my first company and board of directors, appointing four of my best friends, although they really didn't think it was as cool as I did!

I was fortunate enough to find some really close friends upon our arrival at Harvey, North Dakota. The very first person I met was a fellow by the name of Chris. He was walking through a parking lot right behind our retail location, where my grandparents happened to live in the apartment above. I was outside getting some fresh air and noticed him carrying a nerf football. I asked him his name, and we began to play catch. We hit it off right away and had so many things in common. The most surprising was that we would be neighbors in the same apartment building... How cool was that?! Chris and his family were living right below our apartment, so our friendship and bond were extremely strong. He lived with his mother, sister and brother, all of whom I am still close with today.

I want to make a point here to describe the apartment complex in which we were living. These brand-new apartment buildings were low income housing units, something that had never really existed in our community before. I say that out of pride and achievement. Again, my parents were very young when they had me and my siblings. I have two younger sisters, Cherie and Amanda. Amanda was born not long after we moved back to North Dakota. So, here was a family of five with no guaranteed income, trying to start a new business from scratch. So many people like to make the *Field of Dreams* reference when it comes to business - "If you build it, they will come." Nothing could be further from the truth, and let me caution you here, if that is your current philosophy, you need to keep reading this book! That is not at all how building a business works! I never saw any lack of want or need, as my parents did the best they could with what they had.

In those days I spent almost as much time working in my office as I did playing outside. I used to dream of building new businesses and developing new products. I would scribble all the details down in my notebook and carry them with me in my backgammon-briefcase everywhere I went, excited and hopeful for the future with my little leather box of dreams. Little did I know, and thanks to my parents protecting me from the reality, that right above me was the real-life struggle of running a business. As I spent my time working and dreaming about the future, the constant mundane pressures of being a new business - growth, order deadlines, deliveries, repairs, expenses, inventory, marketing, and economy - were actively taking place. I could see that my parents no longer had the same excitement as they once did when they had started, nor did they seem to get along as well as they used to. It didn't really bother me, as I was just a kid and the ignorance of childhood is bliss. Not having any real skin in the game, and not fully understanding the rules of the game, meant those challenges were not my problem. Does any of this sound familiar to you current business owners out there? Well, pretty soon, that was all going to change.

LITTLE ROD'S
GROWING UP

As the family business grew, so did I. My parents had generated success built upon the principle that your word is your bond. I watched my father continue to work longer and longer hours as the service demands grew with the sales. As I got older and made more friends, some of which were female, working late with my dad was not as exciting or cool as it used to be. Thanks to my years spent working and my father's training, I became much more valuable and started to assume actual responsibilities and tasks that I could perform. I started to ask (complain to) my dad, "Why do we always have to work late? This sucks!" He would respond the same way every time. "Because I promised these customers that I would have the work done. You must always do what you say you're going to do." Although I didn't like it, I still admired his commitment and have never lost sight of the principle. Your word is your bond, and if you say you're going to do something, then do it! Simple as it is, it's not always easy to execute. Something that is seemingly lost on today's generation, although I am confident the pendulum will swing back, as long as we help it get started!

Now that I had developed the necessary business acumen, knowledge and skill, this would be my first understanding of having skin in the game. Although it wasn't financial, my parents counted on me being able to get things done, and as a small family business, we couldn't afford to hire more staff. I either helped, or watched my parents take on the extra workload. I had an uncle that would help us out from time to time, and eventually we would work together full-time for years during my high school career. I would say to him, "Hey, Uncle Lawrence, what do you know today?" and he would always reply, "Nothing, the more you know, the more you're expected to do!" He was always joking around, but there is so much truth in that statement. The more you know, the more you're expected to do, since you are indeed capable of doing more. This was something that would impact me both positively and negatively for the rest of my life. Uncle Lawrence and I had a great relationship, both personally and professionally. We both loved sports and music, and had weird but colorful senses of humor. One of his best one-liners was at the end of any family meal when he would stand up, rub his belly and exclaim, "I'm so full, I don't think I have room for a cigarette!" No kidding, at the end of every family gathering, no matter what we were eating, he always finished it with the same statement. It's what I loved about him! When he was the best version of himself, he would light up the room and keep you laughing until you physically hurt. He was also brutally honest. A virtue to be sure, but on occasion, a fault. I'll give you one example where I still chuckle and feel uncomfortable at the same time to this day. We were having a late lunch while on a run of deliveries for the store. We were sitting in a booth at a local restaurant with a mother and her child sitting behind us. I was facing their booth and my uncle was facing away from them. To be fair, the child was misbehaving and demanding money to get a toy from the vending machine. I could see the mounting frustration on my uncle's face every time the child would scream. Finally, he couldn't take any more and, turning, slammed his fist, exclaiming "If you don't slap that kid, I will!" The mother and child stood right up and left. It was uncomfortable, but he had the courage to say what everyone else in the restaurant was thinking. I'm in no way condoning his behavior, but I did appreciate his courage in speaking what was on his mind!

I bet you're wondering how he negatively impacted me. Well, in some ways, the negative impact was still positive. He would always exclaim, "The more you know, the more you're expected to do" with a seemingly joking intent, but in reality, this is how he lived his life. See, when my father teamed my uncle and I together, I was technically the Crew Chief. I was the one who had all the knowledge and who was responsible for properly repairing and installing the products we were servicing. The reason I had somebody working under me despite being years older than me is that I still didn't even have a driver's license. Sometimes this would bother me, because I still looked up to my uncle, especially as an elder. I knew he was extremely intelligent and was one of the hardest workers I knew. Didn't he want to advance or even start something on his own? His answer was always the same... No! He truly didn't want to admit to having the knowledge or capacity to do things in order to avoid the responsibilities that came with it. The fallacy in purposely choosing to know less is that we should always be excited to learn and do more, because that's truly when we grow and become better versions of ourselves! Uncle Lawrence is no longer with us and I love and miss him daily. Although I don't subscribe to his past philosophy, it made a very serious impression on me on not settling for less. I always want to push myself and learn as much as possible!

As our company expanded many times throughout the years, so did my interests. Still a lover of science and sports, I also developed a love for music. This originated from the electronics field, as I was intrigued by amplifiers, speakers and the like. Most of my original 'board of directors' and I stayed friends, and some of the board thought we should start a band. You will probably laugh at the first band name, but it had to be 'Short Circuit' of course. We were just thirteen years old when we played our first gig at the Junior High dance and had a total of six songs on our set list. I spent countless hours wiring up light switch boards (most of the components magically disappeared out of the store's inventory) and sound equipment. We weren't very good, but we had enough passion to make up for our lack of talent. The main ingredient for a startup. Even though most people don't think of a band as a startup business, let me assure you that it is. High startup costs, hours spent honing your craft, physically setting up your stage, logistics, etc. are all part of the entrepreneurial process.

I would continue growing and expanding in the music industry as my father and I drifted further apart. Like any family business, he hoped that one day his children would want to get involved and have the same commitment and drive as he did. As I grew older, the more I knew, the more I could perform for the company. The problem was, I was also wholly committed to my music career and believed that I could do something with it. I could take it beyond the garage. I gave my best to the family business when I had the time, but through the process of becoming a late teen and running my own music business on the weekends, my relationship with my dad became strained. I remember trying to explain to him what I thought I could do and I remember him telling me, "You better get those silly dreams out of your head! The only thing that pays off in life is hard work and time. You can't expect to just make it big overnight!" That wasn't our best day, but two things were gleaned from that for me. One, I had never known my father to be so beat down and bitter before. He was always short tempered, but so was most of my family. It was the way that he seemed to have lost his own dreams and passion, which is what happens in most business owners' lives. The constant barrage of day-to-day issues can force you to lose sight of your bigger goal. Or worse, it can make you forget about it completely. The second thing I gleaned was that I would have to make my own way in life. I wasn't going to be told that "You can't" or "You won't." I was going to give whatever the challenge was everything that I had. If I were to fail, then so be it, but it would be on my terms.

As the stress continued at work, an opportunity came up right after my high school graduation. I had no plans or means for college, and one of the main partners in our music project got a request from a talent agency that a drummer and a keyboard player/singer were needed to fill in for a band out west in our state. I was the drummer and he was the keyboard player. We submitted our head shots and resumés and got the gig. The only problem now was that this would be a fulltime road travel project. I would be touring the United States and finally have my shot in the music world. I decided to take it, but not without putting more stress on my relationship with my father. I went out and played the weekend gig and found the new venture exciting. I gave the new band members a commitment to go in two weeks and gave my family my two-week notice. Needless to say, there wasn't any sendoff party, but this was something I could control. Up until this point in my life, other than the usual high school drama, life had been pretty easy. Being the super cool and smart guy that I was - and if you didn't already know that you could have just asked me, as my greatest attribute was my humility! - I would surely conquer this new business venture. I was clearly smarter than everyone else who had tried it before, so success was virtually guaranteed. This would eventually lead to many new Man...F@#k! moments!

LIVING THE DREAM

I couldn't believe it! Here I was getting ready to head out on the road, seeing places I had never seen before, playing music in front of large crowds, and most unbelievably... getting paid to do it! I truly was living the dream, or at least until I woke up, but we'll get to that.

Because I had worked from such a young age and was blessed with a good growth of facial hair, most people believed that I was much older than I was. This came in handy since I was playing in drinking establishments, and since I liked to drink. Our first stop was Sioux Falls, South Dakota, and after the travel and set up, it was finally time to get up on the stage and perform. The year was 1990 and the music scene had shifted from rock to country, but the two were blended to have a more country/rock feel. I had always been a rock-n-roll drummer, so there was a little pain in the transition, but those clubs were the best-paying gigs. This was the peak of the line dancing craze, so you played what you were paid for. Ironically enough, I would eventually start to really enjoy most of the country genre. Our first set was fantastic! My partner and I had always struggled to find the right caliber of local musicians, so we were so excited to be connected with talent that aligned with ours (I hope you're seeing the overconfident connection here). I got off the stage to the loudest applause I had ever received and believed that a record deal must be just around the corner. I went up to the bar and ordered a cold beer. It was delivered on the house. Could life get any better than this?!

We finished the rest of our sets for the night and the last set was almost entirely rock-n-roll. I was in musician heaven! We shut down for the night, but we were now contracted to play six nights a week, usually two weeks per club. Accommodation was also provided by the club, so after the first night, it seemed as if twenty people followed us back to our room, where more celebrating would take place. Because we finished most gigs at 2:00 am, it was just like getting off work at 5:30 pm from my last job. Needless to say, nobody went to bed after work, and so the next day was always a little rougher than the first, beginning at an early 3:00 pm, which was a little new to me. It was already becoming fall and the sun wasn't around for much that day. It didn't matter, once it was time to get ready for our second night, all the adrenaline returned, and I felt on top of the world. The performance and the after party followed the same trend as the first night. This was the beginning of a pattern, and although it was great for my music aspirations, it would eventually take its toll on my physical and spiritual ones.

Just like during my early days of business, I still traveled with a briefcase. You'll be happy to know that it was no longer a backgammon case, but a full-sized professional briefcase. As you might expect, my fellow band mates also thought I was somewhat of a nerd, but I was indeed a cool nerd and took care of most of the business. I kept a ledger of all income, expenses, and capital expenditures. I created operating and policy manuals for the music equipment and sound operations. Don't forget that my electronics background came in quite handy, so I was sure to make the manual user-friendly in the event that I couldn't be there to operate the system. I can remember being so excited and feeling so cocky, as I was already making more money than when I was working at the store. Of course, much of the income we received was paid in cash, so there was no tax deduction on the wages. We would all later come to know this as 1099 income which would lead to another Man…F@#k! moment. Nonetheless, we continued to travel from place to place.

Once, on our way to a club in Wyoming, we stopped for gas. Our bass player was passed out on the top bunk as we all ran in for some snacks. We paid for the gas and headed back out on the road. About twenty minutes later, I decided to see how our bass player was doing, only to discover that he wasn't there… Man…F@#k! We turned right around and within a few miles of the gas station we saw him jogging down the interstate with a peanut butter cup in one hand and a soda in the other. I still laugh as I'm writing this. Did he honestly think he could run and catch us?! It wasn't a very funny moment until we found him and knew he was safe. It caused a lot of stress for all of us and this would be the first time that we were late for a gig. Still though, it's too funny a story not to share!

The travel would go on with me still having fun but becoming fatigued. There was not much time off from the band, and when you had it, you spent it traveling. I hadn't seen much of the sun in a while. Winter had fully set in and we played at a lot of clubs in ski country. We were once on our way to play a gig at the Million Dollar Cowboy bar in Jackson Hole, Wyoming, when we got caught in a terrible blizzard. The greyhound bus we were using froze up, and we became stranded on the roadside. Once again, we were running late for the gig, and this was one was very important for us. I was standing by the door of the bus to see who would go with me to get help, when suddenly I was thrown into the windshield. Something or somebody had just hit the back of the bus. I ran outside and sure enough there was a big car that had been turned into a capital A, and the woman inside was hurt. We were able to get her out of the car and into the bus, but the engine wasn't running, it was cold, and I was afraid she would go into shock. Man...F@#k!

I bundled up to go get help when I suddenly saw emergency lights in the distance. A local farmer had heard the crash and had called emergency services to the scene. We were happy to get the lady on her way to get help, but as the police arrived, there was a new problem. Although we had pulled over past the shoulder of the road, and even set up reflectors to warn oncoming traffic, the blizzard had made them and us impossible to see. The accident wasn't our fault, but it was discovered that the owner of the bus, who was a member of the band, did not have insurance. Although every month we pitched in, and I had recorded the insurance expense in my journal, he hadn't been paying the premium, but rather just pocketing the money. Now our bus and all our equipment would be towed and impounded, and we would spend the night in jail until we could come up with the premium to renew the insurance policy. Man...F@#k!

We scraped together everything we had and got the policy back in place, but this was making us extremely late, and sure enough we started the gig a full hour late. The owners and managers of the club were not impressed and unlike most gigs, we had to do our stage set up and immediately start playing. We were fatigued and shook up about the accident and arrest, but the show had to go on. We were actually a relatively good band, so by the end of the night all was well in the world musically, but I couldn't help but reflect on my newest business lesson... Trusting others with financial responsibilities and tasks. I suddenly learned firsthand that people don't always do what they say they're going to do - something that my father had always insisted. This created additional tension in the group as we were all out financially, and some didn't have any money left after the insurance raise.

One night, not helped by alcohol, it came to a head between two of the members, where one pulled a gun, and another was thrown out of a picture window of the band house in which we were staying. Man...F@#k! My next lesson in culture, and what it means when you have an energy vampire and a cancer in the group. This also led to a firing and a need to re-hire... I was slowly waking from the dream.

We were able to find a new member for the band and continued our tour. This was already our third replacement member, so I was also in the process of learning the necessity of good hiring practices. We had been offered a six-week sit-down gig in Anchorage, Alaska at a club that was reopening. We were all excited about this opportunity, however, the only catch was that they would fly us there and we would play on house equipment, not our own. As soon as we arrived, it was nowhere near the caliber of equipment we were used to playing on, and for a drummer, your own kit is like a part of you. None of us were happy, and as a result, we did not perform our best. We frankly didn't care anymore, as even the crowd was not what we were accustomed to.

Everyone started adopting a poor attitude towards our music career, and now the more consistent problem of one our guitarists started rearing its ugly head. I won't mention his name here, but he always drank quite a bit... Hell, we all did, but he had a real knack for taking it too far. When his attitude would become poor, he would begin to feel sorry for himself and declare that he was going on a roll. This was also evident when he would switch from drinking beer to whiskey. There is no exaggeration here, he could quite literally drink for over forty-eight hours without sleep and still function. Heavy stress, slurred words and always confrontational. Most disappointingly, he was no longer the amazing guitar player that he was when he was sober. This was another important lesson I learned in business, that no matter the talent, when you don't have someone committed to giving their very best, you will not succeed.

The gig was supposed to last through to New Year's Eve, but

we got so sloppy and arrogant that we were fired on December 22nd. We had planned to take two weeks off after the New Year's deadline, but instead found ourselves flying home early, which was near Spokane, Washington, our band's headquarters. Being from North Dakota, I was hoping to get home and surprise my family for Christmas, but this presented the next problem; since we never completed the gig, the pay was short, and I didn't have enough money to fly home. I called my father to explain that I could travel home but was short of cash. This wasn't the first time I had to call home for money. Although I was making so much more money than I had working in the family business, ironically, I never seemed to have any! We were always improving on equipment and capital expenditures that there never seemed to be anything left after living the lifestyle of a road musician.

Two more lessons were learned from this experience - One, cultural integrity: even when things aren't ideal, you should always perform at your best. I had never been fired from anything in my life before! The second was humility. Maybe my dad did know what he was talking about, and things don't magically happen overnight. My dad was more than willing to send me cash to get home, but since we didn't land in Washington until December 23rd, there was no air travel or car rental available. The only thing we found to get home was a 28' U-Haul truck. My partner from North Dakota and I threw our two suitcases in the back of that 28' box and headed out through the mountains towards home. We encountered a terrible blizzard on the way going through the mountains and were almost in a terrible accident... Man...F@#k!

The roads had been fine when we first started our journey and we were aware of a potential storm that was supposed to be coming up from the south. According to the forecasts, we should have been well on our way home before it hit, but like the weather usually does, we had a terrible surprise just a few hours into the trip. The snow was extremely heavy, and the wind was terrible. I don't know if you have ever driven a 28' U-Haul truck, but the enormous box acts just like a sail! The temperatures had been warm when we left, but once the front moved in, they dropped drastically. This, of course, introduced a whole new element of ice. Now we couldn't see, could barely keep the truck on the road because of the wind, and we started slipping when we entered the winding curves as we traversed the interstate through the mountains. Man…F@#k!

For ninety miles we would take turns driving while the other would stick their head out the passenger window to try and locate the mile markers, since that was the only way we could find the margin of the highway. We did consider stopping, but we were in an area that didn't have a city to pull into and decided that getting off the interstate would be worse. It was definitely one of the worst driving experiences of my life and I live in a state that deals with wind, snow and ice every winter season. Those U-Haul trucks are just not built for that type of travel. We were so fatigued from the lack of sleep and trying to focus on those road markers that we didn't see an upcoming curve. The truck started to slip into a ditch and seemed certain to flip over. My partner was doing the driving at the time and somehow regained control. I am not ashamed to admit that we both stopped and cried for a while, as we thought we would never get home!

After twenty-six hours of travel, I finally made it home and pulled up in front of my parents' house with a 28' U-Haul. My mother had no idea I was coming, so it was great to surprise her and the rest of my family for Christmas. I had two weeks off before we would have to head back on the road. I couldn't wait to see what had been going on in the family business, since I had never lost my passion for it.

THE WAKEUP CALL

After celebrating the holidays with my family, I was excited to get back to the store and see what was going on with the business. As I mentioned earlier, we had started in the electronics industry, but over the years we had expanded into the appliance and furniture industries. This involved moving into multiple larger locations as the business grew. Although the moves and expansions were a lot of work, I had always enjoyed the challenges. I especially liked working on floor planning, construction, new policies and merchandising.

While I was gone, my parents had decided that they could no longer compete in the electronics business. This was during the time of the advent of big box stores. These new, large chains were making it impossible to stay competitive and profitable. The division still provided a lot of revenue, and my parents looked to replace it with something else. They decided on floorcovering. When I returned, they showed me a new location where they were going to expand and add rolls, remnants, and new sample displays. I started to research the business and was immediately drawn to the industry. It still had many of the things I loved, such as math and chemistry. There is a lot of complexity in how these products are manufactured and installed. I remember spending the day thinking about the business potential and coming away with a desire to be involved. The only problem was I was still committed to the music business and we were set to perform in front of a record company at a gig in the near future. I couldn't pass this opportunity up, could I? Plus, we were supposed to play weekend gigs for a couple of local clubs while we were off. Since we had been fired early from our last job, this would help recover lost income.

Another new development was that we had fired the person who owned the bus and would be needing some type of new transportation. My parents attended a gig we played, and I could tell that for the first time my father understood what I was doing. I think he was actually impressed, and maybe even proud of me. I explained our situation, and to his credit, he took me to a bus dealership to look at newer greyhounds that could facilitate our needs. Another lesson in business: since none of us had the credit worthiness to borrow money for the bus, it would be my parents who would take all the risk if we made the purchase by co-signing. Of course, all my band mates were excited and wanted to proceed, but I had reservations from all the turnover we had in the last year on the road. I told them that we would have to make do with the trailer we were using and pulling with our van. If things got better, I would consider following through on the co-signatory, but not until then. I prepared to get back to the road full-time, but not without this subconscious desire to get involved in our newest business venture.

Things seemed to be improving at first. We were as tight as ever as a musical group and were all excited to perform in front of the record company. Even with all the excitement of the upcoming opportunity, I couldn't get the tremendous opportunity my family's business had in the flooring industry out of my head. I just fell in love with it and couldn't help but wonder if my parents would consider taking me back and giving me a chance at partnership.

I really believed I could excel in this business, but still had my musical dream right in front of me.

I distinctly remember one morning when I was waiting outside a gas station, as we were celebrating our day off. As usual, we had been up since the night before, but had run out of beer. I was sitting there, a longhaired rock-n-roll drummer, watching all the business professionals filling gas, grabbing coffee, and preparing to get to work for the day. I felt foolish waiting to get more alcohol from the gas station. Many of these business professionals looked at me with disappointment. I recognized my own disappointment and decided at that moment the party should end. I went back to my hotel room and reflected on the direction of my life. I remember thinking that this was no way to live, and that I would never have a family if I stayed the course. I decided that from there on out, I would play the rest of the scheduled gigs sober. This added a new tension to the group, as I once again became a nerd for not wanting to party. Although I still stand by the fact that I was a pretty cool nerd!

It wasn't long after a performance that I went to my hotel room, holding firm to my commitment by not joining the rest of the group for the afterparty. It was late, our rooms were in a block, and the noise was keeping me awake. I went down the hall to grab a soda from the vending machine when I overheard a couple band members talking about how they should replace me since I was becoming distant and not committing to making the bus purchase. I walked into the room, since the door was propped open, and asked them what they were talking about. Everyone responded with, "Hey, Rod, come join us for a drink," and I asked if there were any concerns about how things were going. The answer, of course, was, "No, everything's going great! Great job tonight!" Another lesson in business: Lack of honesty and communication. Man...F@#k!

I called my dad the next morning and laid out my partnership pitch. He was excited to hear about me wanting to return, and I gave the group my two-weeks' notice. I finally woke up from the dream, and this was my wake-up call. Do I regret not following through with the record company performance? No, I don't! The path and lifestyle were leading to self-destruction, and I am so much happier where I am today. I still continue to play, compose and record music, so the dream is still alive!

THE PRODIGAL
SON RETURNS

I couldn't have been more excited to return home. I discovered a new love for business in the floorcovering industry and was eager to form a new partnership with my parents. Growing up in the business, I had always been mostly involved in the service side. This included warehouse management, delivery, service calls, but also some sales. I had always had the gift of the gab, a trait I inherited from my mother, as she had been the driving force in our sales growth. The day after I returned, I went to our local barber with my long hair in a ponytail, and told him to cut it off. My mother still has this ponytail in her possession today! I went out and bought five suits and new shoes and I was ready to get into management. For me, this was another new startup, and like most people involved in a startup, I couldn't get enough of the work. I spent countless hours learning about the trade and industry, and I spent night after night working overtime to get things just right for our grand opening.

We came out of the gate strong, and within just a couple of years we had expanded the business and moved to a new location. Still having a love for the entire business, I asked if I could take over the sales management for all three divisions. This included furniture, appliances, and flooring. With some reluctancy, my parents agreed, and I immediately started creating new policy, procedure, and systems management practices. I was even given some hiring responsibilities, however, here I was, a twenty-year-old kid, giving orders to thirty- and forty-something year-old employees. As you can imagine, that didn't always go down well, and a lot of tension was starting to form over who was in charge... My parents or me?

Nonetheless, we were seeing great sales growth and starting to develop some sort of culture, which was not a prevalent notion in a small company such as ours. As I grew in confidence, so did my ego. I had taken the company from $600,000 in sales to almost $940,000 in just one year, but things weren't always stress-free! Some of the things I learned on the road were starting to develop in our family business. We needed the right people to grow the company, but we didn't always have the best characters employed. We needed more service team members, specifically in flooring installation. We had employees that were capable of doing the job but couldn't be relied upon to be professional at what they did. I remember it felt like I was running a daycare center.

Even though I was dealing with employees older than me, their personal habits were an impediment. I was living above the store in an apartment we owned, and I had to watch the local bars on main street to make sure certain employees weren't staying out too late. I would often have to run down and plead with them to go home so they could make it to work on time and in the right condition the next morning... Man...F@#k!

I remember the first person I ever hired was a girl who became my first crush. She had just returned to town and graduated with a degree in Interior Design. She would be a perfect fit to our organization, and later, she would become my wife! Angela had always been someone I got along with, and I was excited that she had also decided to return to our hometown. I will never forget her grandfather saying to her, "If you wanted a raise, you could have just asked, instead of marrying the boss." It's a beautiful honesty we have in North Dakota, as both of our families will tell you exactly what they think and always joke around!

After a year of working for our company, Angie and I decided to get married. Together, we have seven children and all of them have been active in some way in our business. As the years progressed after our first three girls, we were blessed in finding out that we would be having twins. Although we were excited about this new development, things were starting to slow down within the business. Not sales growth, but there was now a new power struggle about who was in charge. Did my dad run the company, or did I? The problem in hindsight is that we never established a hierarchy in terms of responsibility. I was acting as the role of general manger, but my parents still owned the company. If I gave orders for the day's business, but my father decided to do something different, obviously the employees would do what he said. This created turmoil and a divide between us once again, prompting Angie and I to consider leaving the business and going elsewhere... Man...F@#k! I loved my parents but couldn't see a future that would allow us to work together anymore. The only logical conclusion I could come up with was either he had to go, or I did. This was one of the most difficult times in my career, because how do you ask the founder of your company to leave, while still in his prime, and not hurt your relationship with you father? Here was my childhood hero, and now I was asking him to leave the very thing he had started... Man...F@#k!

The tension in the air was so thick you could cut it with a knife... literally! But finally, the meeting had to be held. We talked out some of the concerns on both sides, but ultimately, I proposed that either I had to buy them out, or I would have to leave. My dad said, "If you can find a banker to give you the loan, then you can buy us out." I think in hindsight, he never thought I could get the financing! I approached a local bank and gave them my business proposal, and sure enough we could get the loan. I was only twenty-six at the time, but like I have mentioned before, that since I had been in the community for so long and looked so much older than I was, I think this is partially how I managed to get the loan. After we signed the papers, I remember our banker thinking I was in my thirties! I laugh now thinking that I wouldn't have gotten the loan if he had paid attention to how old I actually was!

My parents weren't anywhere near retirement age, but we moved forward with the agreement. It slowly started to dawn on me what I was getting into in terms of debt and responsibility. Talk about real skin in the game... Man...F@#k!

NEW BEGINNINGS

We took over the family business on January 1st, 1999. There was both excitement and nervousness in this new venture. Obviously, we were very young, but my wife and I were ready to get to work. Our original agreement was simply buying the business, not the real estate, as this was a safety clause for my parents. Worst case scenario, if the venture didn't work, they could simply reopen the store without recourse. If things went well, they would have twenty years of lease income at which time we would own the real estate.

We had gotten off to a great start, securing some commercial flooring contracts that helped launch our new company. Again, now feeling more confident (and arrogant) than ever, I felt that nothing I touched could fail. We had expanded into a second location in a different community a couple of years before, another decision my father hadn't agreed to, but we had done it anyway. It was a floorcovering company that was going out of business, but I wanted to expand into larger markets and succeed on a bigger scale. Small time business wasn't the future, or so I thought. I wasted no time in asking our new bank to extend credit to us in order to fully expand that business into a full-scale retail location that included furniture, floorcovering and appliances. This is also when I hired my longtime high school friend Chris, mentioned at the beginning of the book, who had made the arrangement to go to Atlantis. Everyone believed that this was a no-brainer, but like any business, you can grow too quickly, too fast.

Full of my new vigor, I thought the rules didn't apply to me. I was simply smarter than everyone else, and unfortunately, I was surrounded by 'Yes' men. Another good lesson learned here: always make sure you surround yourself with people that see both sides of the equation. It's good to get objections and different perspectives. Overconfidence can kill, things take time to grow.

As you probably realize, we went full steam ahead for the expansion. We leased more space and secured the loans to move forward. We quickly remodeled the space and increased our inventory to become a second location like our original. Inventory showed up and the hiring of new staff began. Even though I had learned the lesson of vetting good quality employees, I was so confident in my decision, I hired most of the first interviewees that came along. I simply wanted to get this business up and running. We got everything into place and even hired an ad agency. We were no longer going to be a small business, so everything had to be on a grand scale. We put a huge advertising budget in place and stocked heavily on inventory. To be honest, our grand opening was a huge success. I was so proud of my decision. I thought I was truly the smartest man on earth. Why hadn't I done this earlier!

As the business grew, so did the debt. Like any startup, we looked past capital requirements and underestimated our growth needs. Although sales were phenomenal, so was the need to finance them. It didn't take long to find out that more working capital was required, so we turned to other unsecured debtors to make it happen. That's when things started to get really tight... Man...F@#k!

Although our sales growth suggested that we had made all the right decisions, our cash flow was struggling. We were financing the payables and the receivables. I also started to figure out that the hiring decisions I made were not right. It seemed that wherever I was not, there were always small fires to put out with employee issues. Again, it was like running a daycare. There were even fights and issues between the landlord and the general manager of our second location. We were simply running out of cash and I was running out of sanity... Man...F@#k!

It was at this very moment that my friend and employee suggested that we go on vacation to the Bahamas to the new Atlantis resort. A place we couldn't normally afford, but thanks to connections in management at the resort, we could get rooms for next to nothing. I really couldn't take the time off, but I went ahead and booked the trip anyway. My wife and I left for this tropical paradise, but there was no way I could relax. What was I doing? Man...F@#k! Everything was going wrong! Needless to say, most of that trip was filled with anxiety and worry. Would we run out of cash? Would the bank call? Would I meet payroll? What if I couldn't? And the list went on and on.

As I mentioned at the beginning of the book, some relief came when the first comedian at the comedy club came out and announced the title of his proposed book. I quickly understood the feeling, and even though all the stress would be waiting for me when I returned, I finally did enjoy myself for a moment. Sure enough, when we returned, there were even more issues and I was now wondering if I knew what I was doing anymore. Perhaps I had made the biggest mistake of my life! Little did I know that things would get even worse.

IT WAS THE BEST OF TIMES, IT WAS THE WORST OF TIMES

Upon arriving back, my friend informed me that he would be leaving the company. I couldn't believe this! How could someone who had helped develop our business strategy be leaving me now when I needed him most? Little did I know that he had other personal issues, but it didn't change the fact that we were in trouble. We entered the year 2000 without any hiccup from the dire "Y2K". This was a concern that most of the world had, and I thought certainly, all my computer software would fail... Well, why not? Man...F@#k!

As we continued to deal with our current struggles, several unforeseen things took place. Early in the year, my grandfather died. This was my father's dad and a chiropractor in our local community for years. Our first startup location for the family business was in his original location, and as I mentioned earlier, my current office is his original treatment office. So, although he wasn't directly involved in our retail business, he did provide the location to start it. He also helped me in my younger years with my music business, giving me my first loan for equipment. He was a great man and is dearly missed.

The next major event was still on the horizon. After getting through losing my friend and employee to relocation, it seemed that we might be stabilizing the expansion. Another set of great friends and family that Angie and I had a relationship with invited us to go with them on a trip to Winnipeg for the weekend. Still not fully humbled by all the things going on, I sent my wife home to get the kids together and pack our bags, as I would stay and take care of some last-minute business. I was always far too busy to help with the kids, so that was her job! (What a jerk…) It wasn't long after she left that I received a phone call from her telling me that I had to go home immediately, something had happened to one of the twins. I could tell in her voice, which was in a tone I had never heard before, that I needed to get home fast.

I remember driving my car down residential streets at what I think was eighty miles per hour. As I approached our home, I saw an ambulance and frantic activity. I also remember the car crunching as I threw it into park long before I stopped. As I got out, I saw Angie, our daughter Chelsey and Spencer (one of the twins) on our sidewalk, all crying and panicking. I glanced over and noticed that my wife's dress was covered in blood and fluid, and everyone was crying. I looked to the ambulance and heard from a distance a voice crying, "Daddy, daddy!" and I realized that my son Quincy was in trouble. As I approached the EMTs that were working on him, I saw this poor little three-year-old with his scalp half torn off, full of blood and injured. I can't describe the feeling, but as you can imagine, it was bordering on horror.

I immediately tried to get to him, but the EMT professionals were holding me back as they had to work on getting him stabilized and rush him to the hospital. I was experiencing the worst moment of my life. Once the group had gotten him into the ambulance and taken him to the hospital, I can't even remember who offered to give us a ride. That is the beauty of living in a small community; everyone was focused on taking care of him and us!

As soon as we arrived at the emergency room, my paternal instincts kicked in. I was sure to solve this problem, as I so arrogantly believed I could. I was almost violent with the hospital staff, insisting that the doctors and nurses let me in to take care of my son. They, of course, did not, and rightfully so. They needed to do the best they could to stabilize him. An emergency helicopter was already on the way. I couldn't believe what was happening! Why was this happening to me? Selfish as usual, I had not realized that my wife and children had just witnessed the event and needed me just as much as I needed them. Moreover, nothing was happening to me, but my son was the victim. Oh sure, we were all devastated, but here was this helpless child, going through all this pain, suffering and anxiety.

I aggressively insisted that someone tell me what was going on and that my son was going to be alright. When I finally asked the doctor if my son would be okay, he gave me a look that I will never forget while he told me he couldn't be sure. They had no idea of what internal damage might exist, they were simply preparing him to be air lifted. As the helicopter paramedics came to take my son, I insisted that I would ride with them. They told me that would be impossible, as they needed to do whatever was necessary to save him. I would only be in the way. Was this the last time I would see Quincy? Was I going to lose my son today?

For the first time in my life, I realized how little control I had over anything. No amount of money or prestige would be able to negotiate me out of this one. I had never been a religious man before, but for the first time in my life I knew that all I could do was pray and trust in God... A God I didn't believe in!

As you would expect in a small community, the local ambulance service offered to drive us to the emergency hospital where Quincy was being air lifted to. It was one hundred miles away and we could get there quicker in the ambulance than if we drove ourselves. The entire time, all I could do was pray and ask God that if someone was going to lose their life today, please let it be me. Here was this perfect and innocent child, and me such a wretch. I would gladly give my life for his. I know all parents can relate to this, but I couldn't have been more sincere. I promised that if my son's life would be spared, that I would seek out God and become a different person.

After hours in the emergency surgical waiting room, the doctors came out and said it was a miracle! There was no internal damage and they were able to put him back together. It turns out that there was a failure on our vehicle's parking system. As they were getting ready to go, one of the twins accidentally hit the gear shift and knocked the van into reverse. Quincy was behind the vehicle and was run over by the car.

This continues to be the worst memory of my life, and no business scenario has ever come close. I spent the rest of the week at the hospital, and with everything going on, I didn't care to check in on the business situation we were in. I studied the Bible and thanked God for the life of my son. To continue the miracle, we were able to take him home in just seven days, though still not fully recovered. I won't turn this into a religious story, but like most vain humans, I was happy to have my son coming home. I was ready to put God back on a shelf and get back to business...

MENTORSHIP,
FRIENDSHIP AND
COMPANIONSHIP...
OH MY!

I met Jack Sears one evening at the local tavern after work. He was sitting at the bar and I sat beside him for a beer. I hadn't seen him before and introduced myself. I was curious about what brought him to our community. We quickly hit it off and found ourselves kindred spirits in terms of our politics, sports, and business interests. Jack was visiting our community prospecting to buy-out a local pharmacy from a couple looking to retire. He explained how his family was involved in running multiple pharmacies in other states and he was looking to relocate to Harvey.

For the next couple of weeks, we continued to meet and form a solid friendship as he waited for his family to arrive and take over the operations of the business. I first met his parents, as his father was the actual pharmacist and Jack would be in charge of building the retail/pharmacy portion of the business. He had such infectious enthusiasm and really got me going in terms of what we could do with our own business. His parents were such wonderful people and had such a refreshing positive attitude that it was hard for it not to be contagious! I remember feeling that they would be such a spark in our little town, and that excited me. Here was someone with the same goals and aspirations of building a big business in a community that wasn't generally looking to grow!

I remember seeing Jack's wife Kelly for the first time, as she definitely stood out from the crowd in terms of appearance. You notice strangers easily in such a small town! They were moving up from Colorado and I remember Jack describing Kelly as his 'Granola Girl'! The first time we met, I had walked into their retail location to see if Jack was around. He had hired us to replace the flooring in his business and I had a quotation for him. Jack wasn't in at the time, and I have to remark on this first meeting with Kelly because later it was revealed that she almost didn't give him the message. See, even back then, I always dressed for success, so I was wearing a double-breasted suit and an overcoat. Kelly informed Jack that someone who appeared to be from the local mafia was looking for him. Something we still laugh at today!

Their family became a huge business in our community, constantly expanding and moving their existing locations. They became great customers and especially friends, as we helped them furnish all their expansions and their personal homes. I remember one occasion when we took Jack and Kelly out for dinner and the check arrived. I quickly picked it up, proclaiming that if they weren't such close friends, I would have been kissing their asses anyway due to all the business they provided. We all got a kick out of that!

They officially settled into our community in 1993. It took Kelly a little time to warm up to me, since Jack and I didn't need much encouragement to go out and enjoy a cold beverage and talk. Having someone who fully understands you personally and professionally is almost therapeutic, but our therapy sessions were pretty frequent. As time passed, our businesses grew along with our families and friendship. Angie and Kelly cultivated a great relationship as well, and we spent a lot of time together over the years, along with our children gathering for family dinners and drinks.

Jack and Kelly were the couple that we were going on vacation with when Quincy had his accident. Like true friends, they met us at the hospital and stayed with us during the whole ordeal.

Jack and I both had second locations in Minot, North Dakota. Since the delivery of the twins was considered high risk, we had to have them at the larger city's hospital. We knew what day Angie was going to be induced, and Jack made sure that he was working close by so he could celebrate with me when the twins were born!

Jack and I always had a great relationship in terms of being a sounding board for each other. We had similar business models, being family-owned and second-generation businesses, specifically with our fathers. We could talk freely and had so many things in common, that no matter what was taking place, we found comfort in each other's struggles and successes. I think it is vitally important to have this kind of relationship when trying to build a business. It's vital to get an outside perspective on how to solve your current struggles. Jack provided great peace and insight, even though he wasn't directly involved in our day-to-day operations. We built our businesses alongside one another for a decade and formed a lifetime bond. Eventually Jack sold his business and moved away from our community, but we still get together as often as we can.

There is a funny story I have to share about Jack. We live in a state that is known for its hunting, and Jack and I decided that we would go goose hunting near his house. His home was in the country and not far from the water. I was settling in down by the water and Jack was above me on a hill. I noticed that a huge flock of geese was starting to settle in and land in our spot. I wanted to keep quiet, but I was trying to get him to notice me... I was whispering, "Jack... Jack..." and pointing up at the geese. Suddenly, he noticed them, and proceeded to unload his shotgun! Now let me be clear, they were so close that I think he could have hit them by swinging his gun above his head, but sure enough after just a couple shots, his gun jammed and we didn't get any geese to fall. We must have spent an hour looking for a part that had fallen off his gun, which was the reason for our unsuccessful hunt. Not until he moved out of his house, did he find the part which had always been in his hunting boot! All this time and it was never lost... I'm still laughing about this, hopefully you are too, Jack!

I had always shared with him my goal of one day writing this book, and I can hear us laughing while clinking our drinks, exclaiming without needing any prompting, "Man...F@#k!"

Am I addicted to drugs? I write this because I had some other great mentors and friends along the way, including more people from the pharmacy business! Our community has always had two pharmacies, and one of the oldest was Krohn's Service Drug. Their business was located right next to our main offices, so when my parents first opened their location, I would frequently sneak over to get some candy. Once, however, I didn't have enough money to buy a candy bar, so I tried to sneak one into my pocket and was found out by the owner. He came to me and asked me to empty my pockets. Much to my shame, I revealed the stolen candy bar. He reprimanded me and let me off the hook, but that moment stayed with me my whole life.

Odell Krohn had been in business for as long as I could remember, and his family was well respected. I was only ten years old at the time of the incident, but the impact of this drove my commitment to integrity! I never wanted to feel that way again! Over the years, as my musicianship increased, their family became some of my biggest followers during my high school career. The biggest impact he had on me was when I moved back to Harvey and we expanded our flooring location. I remember him coming in for our grand opening and exclaiming how proud he was of me and what a tremendous asset to the community this was... It felt like a great reconciliation of my past offense, which I remember so vividly!

Odell was finally ready for retirement and his assistant pharmacist bought him out and took over the business. Gordy Mayer was always someone I knew and had a good relationship with, and he became another person I could talk to regarding business and confidence. I found it funny that after my friend Jack left, I would be confiding in another individual in the pharmacy business! It is always nice to get an outside perspective, regardless of industry, just to know that your daily struggles are not unique. I recently introduced him to my sons after their return home, specifically as a mentor!

But wait... there's more! Since then, Gordy also retired, and a new family moved to town. Chad and Amber Ziegler bought out the pharmacy and have also become close friends. Now I have a new set of pharmacy friends that have the same aspiration of growing our community and businesses. It is nice to keep the momentum going. They have been equally inspirational, and we have so many things in common. As the great Robert Palmer said, "You might as well face it, you're addicted to drugs!" I know it's supposed to be "love", but I couldn't help myself!

My final mention is a fellow by the name of Bob Hale. I first met Bob when we were expanding our second retail location in 1999. He was building a new assisted living retirement complex and we had the opportunity to bid for his project. I met with him in person and we came to an understanding of what our new business relationship could be. This was a very important project for us, since we had just recently acquired the business. We fortunately won the contract and have been serving their company ever since!

Over the decades, Bob and his wife Susie have had an influential impact on our business, both in terms of friendship and commerce. We have done multiple expansions with his group and have become very close friends. I have had a lot of mentorship from Bob. He has always been a great supporter of our cause and spiritual direction and gave me one of the greatest pieces of advice in my life. When we were struggling financially after the fire (which is coming up) and things were tough, I reached out to him as a potential investor. He said that he would be better suited to me as a customer, instead of an investor. Even though I really needed that capital he could have provided, he revealed that I shouldn't give up my equity share. This would prove to be invaluable, even though it seemed hard at the time. He said, "Why would you give up your earnings to someone who hasn't struggled with you in the past... Keep doing what you are doing and when things recover, you don't have to share with someone who hasn't had the same commitment in sweat equity as you!" Very smart advice, and I thank him for it always!

LIGHTING STRIKES

After Quincy's accident, we were overjoyed to be back home with our family. It was a Friday when we had been leaving for the weekend trip, and we returned home from the hospital the following Friday. I had spent the week not worrying about business and focusing specifically on my family and God. Now that my son seemed to be out of the woods, my usual arrogance began to creep back in. I had spent most of the last week reading the Bible and learning about Christianity, so I believed I pretty much had it all figured out! I was, after all, always the smartest guy in the room... What an asshole!

I still had a business to run, so I planned to go into the office the following day to check in on things and work the retail floor. Saturdays were a short day in terms of hours of operation. We closed at 4:30 pm, so I didn't mind going in and stopping by the local pub for an afternoon drink. This was part of my motivation as I felt I had suffered so much by not being able to spend time with my friends and socialize while being at the hospital. I had dedicated an entire week to my family and God, so now it was time for me! How quickly we can lose our faith! It was time to put God back on the shelf, thanks... I can take it from here!

It was a hot August day, and thunderstorms were popping up all day. I remember selling a mattress to a customer right at the end of the day. It was pouring rain. I had them pull into our floorcovering warehouse so that we could load the purchase inside, out of the rain. We got the customer on their way and I had pushed the button to close the automatic warehouse door. I was heading to the electrical panels to shut the lights down for the day when I suddenly felt all the hair on my arms stand up and CRACK! I felt an explosion outside that literally knocked me off my feet. I quickly realized that it was a lightning strike, and my immediate reaction was to check on all our electrical systems… computers, phones, etc. My dad had stopped by and was in the store at the time because we were going to get a beer together after work. Suddenly somebody rushed in and said, "Your roof is on fire!" I remember instinctively grabbing a small fire extinguisher and running up the apartment stairs.

As soon as I got to the top floor, all I could see was that the ceiling was on fire. Funny enough, looking back, I chose to throw the fire extinguisher into the hallway instead of using it the way it was intended. As if that would somehow help! I ran back downstairs and told my dad to call the fire department. We weren't going to put this one out!

The rest of the day and night was chaos and a rollercoaster of emotion. Our local fire department assisted the local community departments who fought the fire until 4:00 am. We drained the local water tower, pumping over 300,000 gallons of water, and still couldn't put the fire out. Thankfully, the rainstorms continued, and all the natural water assisted in finally extinguishing the fire. All the firefighters were exhausted, and we stayed with them throughout the ordeal. It's painful to watch something you have put so much time, blood, sweat and tears into vanish in a single day. We were, however, fortunate that the attached building on our property had been constructed entirely out of steel in 1996. This meant the fire was contained to just our corner three story building, otherwise I'm certain that our community would have lost the entire city block.

Now, I told you that this wouldn't be a religious book, but I would be a fool if I didn't point out the obvious providence in this event! Remember the business was expanding rapidly, which was causing us to bleed cash, my good friend and partner had left the company, and my grandfather had passed away, I was struggling to find new working capital to float the business and was soon to be in major financial trouble. Just a week before, I had nearly lost my son! When one is faced with dire financial options, as hard as it is for me to admit, even suicide seems like a possible solution. Yet here, right in the middle of all the business chaos, I witness a miracle with my son's accident and recovery. Just seven short days later I'm was telling God, "I can take it from here!" And God replied, "No, you can't, here's your sign, you made a promise!" How likely is it that a bolt of lightning struck our building alone, and burnt it to the ground? I remember thinking, "Okay, God, I hear you," and thus began a long faith journey that continues to this day. But that's for another book, so let's get back to this story.

I got very little sleep that morning and returned just a few hours later in the sunlight to assess the damage… Man…F@#k! It was clear that there would be no salvaging the property or inventory. The lightning had hit a transformer in the back of our building, and pieces of it were blown all over the back alley. This was clearly the cause of the fire, and it dawned on me that this could also be providential as we had an active insurance policy. Although still very upset by the loss of a property that we had worked so hard to build, there was comfort in knowing that the capital we would need was on the way. Remember, Angie and I had just purchased the businesses, not the real estate, so the building coverage would go to my parents. We were all feeling some relief, as my parents were aware of our financial struggles and everyone was unsure what to do. I remember joking with my dad one Sunday at our home, "Your rent checks will finally be good!" As a way of helping us out, he had been holding lease payments while we worked through our cash flow issues.

We worked through the insurance process and got our first payment installment. It would take some time to finish up the rest of the details and claim requests, a process that was definitely a Man...F@#k! moment. Anyone that has dealt with an insurance fire claim knows what I'm talking about! For now, however, the initial claim check would take care of the operating costs for our other location and pay back some of the short-term debt we had racked up. It also gave me some time to reflect on the current situation and how we were to proceed in the future. Would we rebuild? Would we relocate? Would we sell? All seemed to be right in the world again, but as we all know, it never stays that way for long.

RECONCILIATION

The business in the location of the fire was obviously still closed. I traveled more frequently to our second location, but was still in the process of dealing with insurance paperwork and reconciling the books pertaining to inventory lost, clearing the checking account, filing operating loss statements for the insurance company, etc. Nobody ever prepares you for the aftermath of a fire… Man…F@#k! It was somewhat refreshing that we weren't actively functioning as a retail location, so we could work whatever hours we chose. This was a freedom that wouldn't be good for me.

As I mentioned in the previous chapter, 9,000 square feet of the real estate we owned was constructed out of steel. The property had smoke and water damage, but the structure was intact. It was also the location of my office at the time and at least I had an alternative place to work. There was cleaning up to do, removing the old flooring, clearing out the inventory, smoke damage restoration and new paint, so there was plenty to keep busy with. Without a deadline, it was easy to call it a day early and enjoy a cold beer after work. This activity included most of the employees I had been working with at the time. Having newfound capital, DRINKS WERE ON ME! This became way too frequent and started to take a toll on my family life, specifically my marriage. My son Quincy was still healing from the accident, and there was plenty of work to do around the house. My excuse was always,

"I've got to go down and take care of business," but we both knew that meant working two-thirds of a day and celebrating all that was accomplished. This meant that during a usual day, I would see my kids for thirty minutes in the morning then kiss them goodnight, as they were asleep when I got home. I'm not including this with pride, this to me was one of the lowest points in my life. I had been given so many opportunities, even a miracle, and I chose to squander it instead... Man...F@#k!

One night, I was working late at the office, and I received a bank statement showing that our main checking account was overdrawn. This couldn't be, as when I checked the account, my computer software showed a positive balance. During the reconciliation, I noticed some things I couldn't balance, and they appeared to go much further back than just a couple of months. I started running journals and reports going back nearly two years. To my horror, I found that multiple months of checks that had been processed after our normal cutoff date had not been posted. Nearly $70,000 worth of checks were not reflected in my computer balance. Furthermore, no checking reconciliation had been done for over seven months. I remember feeling like the 'no insurance on the bus' band days, where I had trusted somebody to take care of things and they hadn't done so.

Two different employees contributed to this debacle, and neither of them were in my employ any longer, so it was just me and this terrible new problem. All this time I was thinking that the fire would be a blessing, not knowing that the trouble I thought I was in was just the tip of the iceberg... Man...F@#k! To add insult to injury, I received notice from my insurance company that they had paid me the maximum allowance for our inventory loss. This couldn't be, we had lost about $80,000 more than they had repaid. I argued and pointed out my policy coverage, only to discover another horror show. When we had expanded our second location and increased the insurance coverage for the contents of that location, we failed to mention that there wasn't sufficient warehouse space at the specific site, so most of the backup inventory was warehoused in our original location, which had burned down. The insurance coverage for the additional inventory was assigned to the location that hadn't. I argued until I was blue in the face, but there was nothing I could do…We were under-insured. Here I was, a young business owner, with barely $70,000 of net worth when I had started the company, now with an additional $80,000 loss. I never went to college or studied accounting, but I'm pretty sure that puts us in bankruptcy. This was beyond…Man…F@#k!. This was devastating!

I remember going home after spending an hour crying and screaming at work, as I had no idea what I was going to do. How would I tell the bank? How would I tell my parents? How would I tell my friends? More importantly, how would I tell my wife?! She took one look at my face and knew something was wrong. Expecting me to come home from another short workday celebration, she could tell that I was stone-cold sober. She grabbed me and asked, "What's wrong?' and I immediately broke down. I explained the discoveries I had made, and we cried together until we finally fell asleep, exhausted and heartbroken.

I woke up the next morning, and my new struggle of depression and anxiety began. The first thing that entered my mind as soon as my eyes opened was, *I don't want to be here.* Not just in this situation, but in this life. I can't tell you the horrible thoughts that went on for me during this period. A further new development was that I didn't want to get out of bed and face reality. I lost all motivation and confidence in myself, which looking back was a good thing. I really needed to be gut-checked and humbled, and ultimately the lesson learned from this ordeal truly did make me stronger. The cliché applies: "What doesn't kill you makes you stronger!" But back to the struggle.

Once I finally got my ass out of bed and faced the day, I began to brainstorm a way out. I had used the insurance money to pay back operating lines of credit, but now as the checks cleared after the reconciliation, I was beginning to max them out again, and I wasn't even operating one of our main locations. Something had to be done, and fast. I decided that I would contact my general manager in our second location. He had been with me when we first opened as a floorcovering store. I suggested that he could buy out the flooring division, and since the 9,000 square foot property that hadn't burned down could be restored relatively quickly, I would arrange semitrucks to haul all the furniture and appliances back to the original location and get it reopened. This was the best way I could think of to recover cash and profits... Reopen and get selling! To my surprise, after laying out the terms of the deal, my manager was interested. Thanks be to God, I remember thinking. I could finally get rid of my second location, which had been draining us of all our money, and get rid of managing the additional employees. Angie and I had talked about selling our home and moving to that community, but our hearts weren't really in it. So here was my chance to get everything I wanted... Stay in my hometown, get my original business back up and running, sell off my second location, get rid of most of my daily headaches, and slowly but surely... recover. My manager had accepted my agreement and had a partner and the financing in place. We would close the deal the following week. I finally started to feel a sense of relief.

The following week arrived and just days before the close, I was still working on the finishing touches of the remodel in our main location. I heard the phone ringing, which was odd, since we had been closed for over a month. I answered, and it was my manager. "I've got some bad news. My partner got cold feet and the bank won't give me the loan on my own. They will if you cosign, though." What? Man...F@#k! If I cosigned, I would be giving up control and still hold the debt! I said, "This is crazy, we need to set up a meeting with your bank." I set the meeting for the original day we were supposed to close. Nothing could be done in terms of the sale unless I cosigned. Again, I thought how could this be happening? I had had enough! I decided right there that since all the arrangements had been made to move the furniture and appliances out of that store, I would simply close and liquidate the flooring division. This, however, created all sorts of new expenses, such as unemployment claims, more advertising for the liquidation, lower profit margins, and having to stay open to facilitate the installation of the product, as we were usually booked eight to ten weeks out. I would have to remain open for another three months after closing, just to tie up the loose ends. Great, another business location spending money on operating costs, but not taking in revenue... Man...F@#k!

After all the had dust settled, and there was a lot of dust, I shouldn't have to explain that things were not good. Still working with the insurance company, since we did have loss of business, it was amazingly difficult to collect on. At this point it was the only thing keeping me afloat, and it was ending very soon, as our grand reopening was looming. The next step was for me to meet with the bank. This was going to be one fun meeting... I should have changed my name to Lucy, because, "Someone's got a lot of 'splaining to do!" Man...F@#k!

No details are needed to explain the outcome of the meeting. Things were not good, and after everything was cleared in terms of insurance, we had less than 10% equity. The bank did not advise bankruptcy, but our accountants did. I still feel that is the worst word in the world. It has so many bad connotations and applications. Without a doubt, filing bankruptcy meant failure, even if it was just to reorganize. Angie and I talked about it, which by the way was quite rare during this period, and we decided we would not choose that alternative. We negotiated a very limited line of credit with our lenders, reopened our original location and started over, completely bare bones. Our retail salesforce consisted of Angie and I, two low-paid delivery/warehouse employees, and a subcontracted flooring installer. Since we were on such a limited budget, it was extremely difficult to find and hire good help, so without boring you with more details, financial struggles weren't the only struggle… Man…F@#k!

Angie and I took turns working every other week, six days a week. This meant that we never had more than Sunday off together as a family. This continued to take its toll on the kids and our marriage. Even though we worked together every day, we really didn't spend any time together. We did our work, and when we did talk, we fought. I will take most of the blame here, as with all my confidence lost, I became bitter and resentful. I regretted ever wanting to be in business, and completely doubted my ability. It was the law of attraction: I would simply expect the worst to happen, and sure enough it would. I didn't even like myself at this time, and lost touch with most of my friends. Who would want to be around a loser like me? Man…F@#k!

THE HITS KEEP COMING

So here we are, trying to make our way back from virtually nothing. I got solicitations every day from unsecured debtors looking to set us up with fresh working capital. However, that had been part of the problem in the first place! But what do you do when you haven't cashed your paychecks for months, and still can't meet payroll and other expenses? You sign up for more unsecured credit. Remember, this is now well into the year 2001, and there were clauses with all this interest free money stating that if you carry the balance over certain limits, your interest rate can climb up to 24%. Add this to the list of challenges we were going through, and the hits kept coming! Soon we are sitting with over $100,000 of unsecured debt, most of it costing over 15%. Instead of reducing expenses and cash flow, they were increasing. Not to mention that the amount of real estate lost to the fire was around 14,000 square feet, so our business model had completely changed. Floorcovering was always our dominating division, representing over 42% of our total revenue. It was one of the highest profit divisions. We had always held a large number of in-stock rolls and remnants. At our peak, we had over two hundred rolls and remnants on hand! Now, even though we belonged to a buying group, which allowed us to get the equivalent of roll pricing without the commitment to stock, psychologically it looked to our customers like we were out of the flooring business. Ever since we had opened, we had been primarily a stocking dealer, with sample cut order business being only a small part of our sales. I knew our new business model of less stock could work, but couldn't get the customers to buy in. It took us more than seven years to rebuild a business we once dominated... Man...F@#k! Now we were trying to rebuild our business, almost as if we had just started from scratch and were dealing with a new financial crisis. What a fun time!

By this time, our marriage was shaky. When we talked to each other it consisted of fighting and crying, and frankly I don't think we liked each other anymore. Thank God we still loved each other, or I probably wouldn't be talking about my wife. I also thank God for getting us through this time, because Lord knows she should have got out. We went through so many struggles together, for such a long time. We didn't start to turn the corner until 2007, and even then, it would take until 2010 to fully get out of this funk. That's a long time when your wife and best friend is also your business partner, and for any of you in the same situation reading this, I know you understand!

Also included in our top ten countdown was the continued struggle to find good employees. Our turnover rate was horrific, as either we fired employees, they quit, or they simply just never showed up for work! We had guys that looked like you should be afraid to have them in your home, and in some cases, you probably should have! But what could we do? Angie and I couldn't do the deliveries after hours (side note, it was actually discussed) so we did the best with what we had. I always knew that the complete success of a company would ultimately come down to its staff. Although we didn't have many employees, I had a vision of what our company could look like. After the expansion and the second location debacle, I knew that moving forward would require one location that could expand its trade area in order to increase business. But with the continued financial challenges, I was having a hard time seeing, or even remembering our original vision. Suddenly, I knew exactly how my father felt the day he snapped at me about my music dream. Here I was, angry and bitter just as he was. I had to get out of the mess, but how?

All this was happening right after the tech bubble and continued through the housing crisis. These did have an impact on our business, but the real purpose of mentioning this was the country-wide debt crisis. Many individuals and companies went after these easy, unsecured loans, and were now paying unmanageable interest rates that ranged from 14% - 29.99%, hence the advent of debt-management companies. We were included in this mess. After looking at all the options and directly contacting the lending institutions, there was no negotiating. As was mentioned earlier, bankruptcy was suggested, but we couldn't go that route. Also, to be clear, these were lines of credit, not credit cards, but the terms were quite similar and equally devastating. So, we reached out to a firm that managed exclusively commercial debt and began a process of consolidating and negotiating settlements. If you have never gone through this process, this is the ultimate Man...F@#k! To start the negotiations, you first must go into default. This triggers a very intense moment of debt collection calls, and even some legal action. We had to issue power of attorney and even involve our local attorney to facilitate us through this. Although we were starting to settle and pay off the unsecured debts, it was tanking our personal credit scores. Even though we have always been a subchapter C corporation, in many cases the unsecured debt was looking for personal guarantees. We went through a long period where even financing an automobile became difficult unless we worked with our local bank. At times I felt like a criminal, which was the way we were being treated. These were large banks, which I will leave unnamed, but honestly, we could have negotiated better rates from the mafia! To me, the real criminal activity was the expectation of charging or collecting debts for 30% interest, when even at that time, prime was under 7%. I would take those margins any day! Thank goodness some of that got cleaned up in Congress, but it really was painful getting through that process... Man...F@#k!

THERE'S A LIGHT AT THE END OF THE TUNNEL... I HOPE IT'S NOT A TRAIN!

I think I've given enough examples of how between the years of 2000 and 2007, things weren't going so well. You might even be asking yourself at this point, why am I reading this and what could I possibly learn?! I assure you there is a light at the end of the tunnel... I'm just hoping it's not a train!

I know I keep saying I don't want to make this about religion, but for me, it has been a very significant change and part of my life. Ever since my son's accident, I have been on a journey, both trying to seek out God, but also trying to disprove him. I have always been a lover of science and was taught through math and electronics to think logically, so for most of my younger life, I felt that religion was for fools. My encounter with the possibility of losing someone I loved so much, even more than myself, struck a chord with some of the details and stories I had been familiar with in terms of Christianity. As a matter of fact, it was the very prayer I offered up for hours that terrible day, "That if someone was to lose his life, please let it be me!" I couldn't help but think that only love could be willing to make such a sacrifice, and if I was capable of that kind of love, how much greater would God's be? I won't dwell on this for too long, but after the reassurance that God wanted me to continue my journey, by sending down a lightning bolt and completely changing my course of business, it really has been a big part of my story.

In 2007, after years of study and doubt, I finally decided to be confirmed in the Catholic Church. In 2008 I attended a spiritual retreat, and really did find peace there. For me, the biggest business change that came from that was a shift in management philosophy. Up until this point, I had mirrored my dad's philosophy, which was more of a micromanaged style, with a no-screwing-around attitude. Things were very disciplined, and work wasn't really fun. Of course, neither were the things we were going through, but something had to change. Another major epiphany was how I really needed to get back to focusing on my family and my marriage. I came out thinking that if I lost it all in terms of business, I really could not care anymore. I would gladly live in a cardboard box, as long as I had my family. I also knew that things had to change when it came to staff. It was paramount now that we find the right people, people that aligned with these same values, or this shift in culture would not be sustainable.

I was locked away for three days, a testament to my wife who continued the struggles at work while I was getting myself right. She knew it was exactly what I needed. The funny thing is, I knew deep down that when I went back to work on the Monday, nothing in the outside world would have changed. There would be money problems, employee issues, and the list goes on, but for some reason, I didn't care. Not because I no longer cared about my business but because I cared about things in the right order for the first time in my life. I realized the only thing I could control was myself, and I would simply give everything my best, and nothing more could be given. I would put my trust in God and have faith.

So, in a strange way, I actually cared more, but this time about the right things.

My first order of business was to apologize to my wife and family. We had a long discussion about how things would be changing, and I asked them for forgiveness. The next item on the agenda was talking to my staff, which included letting some of them go. I started with our subcontracted installation group. I always had a grand vision that the ideal business model for floorcovering was to have employed installers. We had organized this group since its inception and treated them like employees. We scheduled work for them every day, stocked their needed tools and supplies, and even ran their billing and collections through the store. The problem was, with all we did, they really weren't employees, nor did they act like it. They would take time off with little or no notice, or not show up at all. We had guys that would lie to the customers and us, not show up to the job sites, and worst of all, they did not share the values that we had as a company. No kidding, I once received a call from a customer asking how my installer's test results had turned out? I fumbled a bit on the phone because I had no idea what they were talking about. They proceeded to tell me, in detail, about the tumor that was found on his spine and they were wondering if it was cancer. He had been off the last couple days seeing the doctor, they told me. I just about had to see a doctor myself from the stroke I was about to have! I went ahead and perpetuated the lie, by answering that we think he will be fine. This of course was complete bullshit! I immediately got into my car to look for him, and sure enough, his van was parked behind the bar. I rushed in and called him outside. I am not a big guy, nor am I a fighter, but I concluded that the only thing this guy would understand was an ass kicking! He then of course played dumb and laid out another pile of excuses, but never did come outside. This was during the infamous 2000 - 2007 period, before

I found some peace, but this was the stuff that had to come to an end... Man...F@#k!

So, I sat down with the group I was working with and let go the guys that I knew would never be able to share in our vision, which included the liar in the previous story! This really hurt, because business was starting to come back, and we were busy in terms of schedule. I sat down with a couple of guys I felt could manage the transition of what I envisioned for the company, and calmly asked for their assistance and willingness to commit. I was pleasantly surprised that they were willing and understanding of what I was looking for. Maybe there was something to this new strategy! I then looked at our delivery/warehouse personnel. Nobody in the group at the time should have stayed on, but I couldn't let everyone go. I chose the lesser of the two evils and went on the lookout for the right fit for these positions. Now remember, there was no magic wand that made everything happen overnight. As a matter of fact, it took a couple years to really start putting the right people in place, but once I was able to see my original dream again, and regain some confidence, things really did seem to turn around.

There really is something spiritual and universal in terms of the power of belief and positivity. When you are constantly negative and expect negative results, sure enough they seem to manifest. But once you shift your thinking into positive thoughts and expectations, sure enough they manifest as well. With this new shift in culture, we became a more positive group. The workplace became fun again, not without challenges as they will always exist, but it was the way we reacted to them that changed our perspectives. My wife and I seemed to fall in love again, and as a result we had two more children. Our business really began to grow and no surprise, so did profits and cash flow. We finally were seeing the light at the end of the tunnel, and I could confidently tell you it wasn't a train, it was daylight and freedom!

DON'T GET ME WRONG...
WE LIKE TRAINS!

I'll get to the point of the title of this chapter later, but first I want to start with the power of gut instinct. As I said, years were passing by as we slowly but surely shifted to becoming a better company. One day, however, I had an employee that just needed to go. I needed somebody that could manage our service department, as again business was growing and in need of additional management. I was eating lunch and was in the process of leaving the restaurant, when I noticed a young couple sitting near the entrance. My wife and I went out the front door and crossed the street. This is a place we still frequently eat at and is across the street from our main retail store. Right before we were going to enter our store, I said to Angie, "I'll be right back." I walked back to the restaurant and sat down with the couple. I asked the man if he was possibly looking for a job. He kind of blushed and answered that he was. He had recently left his old job but hadn't sent any resumés out yet. I proposed that he come and work for us and explained a brief job description and wages. He stopped by after he finished lunch and toured the facility and decided he would take the job. I had a feeling just by looking at him, that he had positive energy, and although I was sure he had never worked in our industry before, he would be someone that was teachable. He started the very next day.

60

He worked the first week for us, which was short since he started on a Tuesday. Things seemed to be going well and he caught on quickly to all the mechanical and detail work. I liked his spirit and jovial attitude, and he was fun to be around. The next week I noticed that he wasn't quite himself. His work ethic remained, but something was clearly bothering him. He just didn't have the same fun and light spirit that he had the week before. Finally, I approached him after a couple of days. I asked how he was liking his job and if there were any questions or concerns I could address. He was extremely quiet, and I knew something was wrong. Finally, he said to me, "Rod, I just don't think I can continue working here." I was shocked by this, since he had only been with us for less than two weeks. I politely asked that he explained what he didn't like about the job, or whether I had offended him in some way. He insisted on not talking about the reason, just stating that he would finish the week and go. Something was so strange about this, and I literally pleaded with him to explain, which he eventually did.

I had started him in our warehouse and delivery team. I had a crew chief appointed above him, who had been with us for quite a while. He was a good employee, but not great. Of course, he knew our systems and policies, so until the new guy could get trained, he couldn't advance. He started explaining. "I actually love what I'm doing for you, and things really started out great! But last week when we were on the road, we got ahead of schedule. I thought, boy, I will make a good impression on Rod for helping to increase productivity. But my supervisor started just driving around the country slowly, wasting time. Finally, I asked him whether we shouldn't get going to the next stop, and he said, 'No way, if we get back early, we'll have to do more work.' That really bothered me. The next day we followed a similar schedule, and then when we got back to town, we stopped by his house, and he took a trade-in item inside that was in really nice shape. When we got back to the store, he told me to confirm that the item was in poor shape, and that we disposed of it at the dump. I just can't lie and cheat you, Rod." I knew instantly that this was my man! Finally, somebody who understood and was aligned with our values. I wouldn't let him out of the office until he promised to stay. I told him if he could finish out the rest of the week, by Monday I would have a replacement to work underneath him and promote him to crew chief. There was a risk here, since there was so much more he needed to learn, but this was the spark that really lit the fire for our cultural change. This was the future of our business, people like this. I scurried to find a replacement and let the long-time, older employee go at the end of the week.

Again, nothing happens overnight, but this guy took the bull by the horns and completely transformed our productivity. He was always looking at ways to improve efficiency and constantly looking to learn. He had tremendous mechanical skills and would shortly be trained to become our appliance technician. I then invested in sending him to training seminars and online courses. In just a couple of years, he would be promoted to Service Manager and Assistant Store Manager. He is still with us today, and currently holds a spot on our board of directors. He is still his goofy self and will happily tell you that the real company turnaround was because of him. In some way, I think it was, at least culturally!

As things grew, we needed to continue to hire, and we were still working on getting the installation group on board. We were able to find a fulltime salesperson, who I'm happy to say is still with us today. She can constantly be counted on for any task and has really grown as an individual. The final hurdle for us was converting our flooring installation team from being subcontracted to actual employees of the company. I had implemented a new policy whereby they had to follow a procedure and a standards/guidelines manual. By now they all wore company uniforms but still weren't on the payroll. We had always struggled with this group, as it is one of the most demanding positions. At one point we were running three two-person crews and trying to develop consistency in performance and procedure, as some past members would treat every job like a competition. We couldn't have that type of division in our company.

It became evident that most of the turmoil was coming from a single individual. The problem was, he was the best detail installer we had. Could I let this guy go, and still sustain the growth we were experiencing? Angie and I could finally afford to take some time off, and I usually like to read on vacation. I bought a book call *The Energy Bus*, and this is where I learned and borrowed the term 'Energy Vampire'. It was evident in everyone's body language that as soon as his voice was heard, everyone slumped and got quiet. He was our 'Energy Vampire!' Everything had to be focused on him… He was the best, he worked the hardest, challenged every policy change, and the list goes on and on! I knew deep down that he had to go, and after reading the book, I was confident that things would work out for the best. Sure, there would be some pushback - that was the kind of person he was - but nothing that would affect us too much. The upside was that we would finally get rid of the last of the cancer, and it has more than paid off! I rearranged the crew chiefs and put the right people in the right positions, and I can tell you that they are still flourishing. So, if you find yourself in a similar situation, don't hesitate to act! Most of our current employees have been with us for nearly a decade and I'm happy to say our turnover rate is close to zero.

Okay, so I have gotten a little ahead of myself in the book! I will talk about more of our cultural shift later, but I needed to lay the foundation about how we were starting to get the right people in the right positions. We were growing our business in the commercial flooring sector, as we could team up and work as company group without internal competition. This gave us a unique advantage in procuring large job site projects and gave us the ability to get the work done quickly and efficiently. This happened over the course of many years, but we were quickly establishing ourselves as a small company that could compete in a large market!

One day, two customers walked into our retail location - I will refer to them as Jack and Jill. I approached them with my usual pitch and assumed that they were husband and wife. I got an immediate response of "Nooooo!" and still laugh at this today as they were simply coworkers! I found out that they represented CP Railroad and were looking to buy up some property in town to help facilitate their growth opportunities and employment needs. I continued to talk about what we could do for them, and eventually developed a new and long-lasting friendship.

Our state of North Dakota had been blessed with finding even more oil than originally projected out in the Bakken field, and the normal transportation at the time was rail cars. They were experiencing the need for additional employees, and Harvey had always been a main depot for the company. They talked to me about the opportunity for our business, and it all seemed too good to be true! Not long after our meeting, I received an order for multiple products and services, but never having done business with them before, I was reluctant to feel too confident and secure. Could this be real? I accepted the orders, and the volume of business was overwhelming. They needed multiple products and had very demanding deadlines. I soon discovered that we couldn't facilitate the demands with our current warehouse space, so I found a different location to lease. Ironically, this would be a building from one of our first location expansions in our early years, so I was very familiar with the real estate. The orders came in quickly and were substantial. This was exciting for sales, but would we be able to collect? I had been down this road before by the promise of "big business" and had been burned. Either this would catapult us into an extremely new and exciting business relationship, or if we couldn't collect, it could bankrupt the company. To cut a long story short, we began a very strong business relationship that remains today, even though they no longer have the real estate model in place. We couldn't have done this expansion without the right people in the right positions! Though it was extremely challenging, it was extremely rewarding, both in terms of business, but also in terms of management. Everyone had to be on their best game, and we seemed to knock it out of the park!

We had worked hard to facilitate all the quick demands, as they were also under deadline pressure, which meant so were we. We received an extremely large furniture order and filled up our newly leased space. As we were waiting to fulfill delivery orders, the worst possible thing that could have happened, happened!

The property we leased had apartment space above it. One cold February day, I suddenly heard sirens and they seemed to be heading right for our store. Had somebody been hurt? I went out the back of our property, as the newly leased property was just across the street and noticed that fire trucks were pulling up to our new warehouse location. It seemed to have been a simple kitchen fire in one of the apartments, but quickly escalated into a major fire. Surely this couldn't be happening again... Man...F@#k! Sure enough, it didn't take long before the entire building was engulfed in flames, and I quickly realized that all the inventory we had stored for this new contract would be lost! I instantly called my contacts and explained the situation. The response I got was not good. The response was, "We will be ready for delivery in two to three weeks, so if you can't fulfil your promise, we will have to get it elsewhere." How could this be? It would be virtually impossible to get new inventory in time, but I had to make it happen. This was a six-figure contract, and the thought of a refund would have been just as detrimental as not getting paid. I immediately got on the phone with our vendors and explained the situation. Much to my relief, everyone pitched in and got the new replenishment order expedited.

As you are probably realizing, I really don't like fires! For most people, including many in our community, they thought that another fire was just a gift. If you have ever been through one you would know that you are only compensated for the cost of your loss. None of your profit is considered. We had some personal items in the building which were not included in the coverage, so once again this would be accounted as a loss. Not to mention the amount of time our team members spent handling and stocking the warehouse. When all was said and done, this would be another $10,000 loss due to fire... Man...F@#k!

We now had a loss of space and no way of warehousing the new incoming order. Our staff were awesome at working the problem, as we donated all our used items in our clearance center to the people who lost their apartment residence and personal items in the fire and made room for the new incoming freight. We were able to cram all this extra inventory into our limited space and get our obligations to CP Rail fulfilled. It was a stressful time, but a testament to having the right people on your staff. This also brought about thinking towards the future. If we were going to continue growing our business and current contracts, how would we facilitate it? We had only just expanded into the property that was lost in the original fire of 2000. We were finally recovering from that loss and had expanded a new flooring warehouse on half of the lot in order to make room for our commercial flooring growth. Business had improved and so as a gesture of good will, we developed the front half of the property into a community park, in which a staff member and I planted sod to ensure the park went into immediate effect. We started to look at options for a new warehouse location, and quickly realized that expanding on to our own property was the most logical option. This would include tearing down the two-year-old park, but generated the best scenario for efficiency, keeping everything under one roof. I remember the day I watched all the work we had done in the park being torn down and removed, all the while thinking... Man...F@#k!

Our new group of dedicated employees worked their asses off and made everything happen. So here we were, seeing a light at the end of this tunnel, and it was actually a train! As I'm sure you can imagine... we really liked trains!

I WENT FOR A DRIVE

We were finally building the momentum we needed to get to the next level. Our shift in management philosophy, culture, policy and procedure was really starting to pay off. As I knew we were ready and our floorcovering division was growing, I decided to rejoin the buying group of which we were once a part. I had joined Carpets Plus back when they first came into being in 1997. The co-owners of the group had worked for Mohawk Industries before starting this new company and I knew them from when I had first returned to the family business in 1991. We were a Mohawk Color Center member when I first came back to manage the flooring division and attended two of their conferences in 1992 and 1993. Ron and John were in management for Mohawk at the time, and it was hard not to get fired up about what was going on in the company back then. They were growing at an unbelievable rate and it was exciting to be a part of it. After the two executives left Mohawk to start the new buying group, I knew that it was the right decision to join up with them. We had just expanded into our second location in 1997, and at the time, this would give us the buying advantage and private label protection we needed in the larger and more competitive market we had entered. Our relationship was good and working really well for us, but when we went through the fire of 2000 and eventually realized the trouble we were in, we had to leave the group, as we could no longer afford to pay the membership fees. Remember, we had completely changed our business model and sales had plummeted, so it simply didn't make sense to stay in the group at this time.

Now that things were changing, I reached out and contacted the group, expressing my desire to rejoin. We were welcomed back with open arms and extreme amounts of enthusiasm! I was asked to attend one of their conferences right off the bat, which I had never attended in the previous years I was a member. I had high reservations to commit. Coming out of the struggle we had been in for so long, I really paid close attention to additional costs. Could I afford this? The air fare, the hotel room, the conference fees, etc. all came to mind. I really struggled with making the decision, but finally decided I would attend. The theme for their conference was "Drive." I booked my trip and made my way to Atlanta Georgia for my very first visit. When I landed at the airport, they had arranged transportation to get me to the hotel. Three other members arrived at the same time I did, and we rode together on the shuttle transportation. I was quiet and reserved right away, not my normal state, but the other members were so excited and couldn't wait to get to know me and our company. It was a great ice breaker, and I could sense that being part of this group was not just a business relationship, it was more like family. Being a family-owned company, this made me feel right at home! I checked into the hotel, and still not knowing many people, wondered what this was all about.

The next morning, I made my way to the conference halls. There was an intense agenda. Many people think attending a conference is like taking time off from work, but let me assure you that they are plenty of work, but in a good way. The first speaker would be Ron Dunn, one of the founders of the buying group. As soon as he began speaking, I knew I had made the right decision! I won't bore you with all the details, but I was inspired. He mentioned so many things that either I was already doing, or things that I thought would be good business concepts. I even teared up a couple of times as some of his remarks really hit home. He talked about family businesses and some of the struggles that go along with them. We had finally grown our business volume to just over $1.4 million and he remarked that anyone doing business over a million dollars was really doing something. This gave me a boost of much-needed confidence and motivation. During that morning opening talk, I wrote down a goal to grow our business to over two million that very year.

We broke for fifteen minutes until the next session would begin, and the first thing I did was call my dad. I was so overwhelmed with emotion that I wanted to call and thank him for my opportunity to take over the family business. Though we were now doing things quite differently from when my parents had owned it, I never lost sight of what they had gone through in terms of taking the risk to start something from nothing. I had never attended college, so really all my business, sales and work ethic training came from them. Even though our relationship wasn't always good, as working with family is very difficult for those of you who have never done it, many of the challenges we faced together had prepared me for this moment and I knew things were really going to be different. I almost wanted to get on a plane and return home, just to get to work! If all I got out of this conference was just the first couple of hours, it would have been worth every penny spent to get there! Obviously, I returned for the next session, and things would only get better as I heard more speakers and was given the tools needed to get our business to the next level. I left Atlanta bursting with confidence and so many new ideas that I had discovered while networking with other members of the group. I was determined to implement these changes and to meet my new sales goal. I am proud to say that we did finish that year just over the two million mark, and I was humbled and surprised when I returned the following year to have won an award for the highest sales growth in the upper Midwest region.

I don't write this to brag, but to assert the power of positive thinking and the benefit of being around the right people. Success breeds success, and you must believe it to achieve it! I have never missed a conference since attending my first, and want to assure you that no matter what industry you are a part of, if you get the opportunity to attend something similar, you need to do it for yourself. There is tremendous power in being in a room with like-minded people!

One of the things that I gleaned from this experience was the need to really start a cultural theme. I came up with the term 'Professional and Personal Excellence' and began to hold weekly sales meetings and monthly staff meetings. I developed a concept that would challenge our staff to conduct themselves, both personally and professionally, and to excel at everything they do! I explained that this wasn't just customer interaction, but how you treated your waitress, co-workers, spouses, etc. This also would lead to a new slogan for us internally, 'Be Remarkable Today'. I have this posted above every warehouse exit to remind our service team to exceed our customers' expectations. Doing your job to the best of your ability is expected, and we should take no simple reward in that. Going above and beyond, and giving the customer an exceptional experience is the goal. Having a great and fun-loving attitude is what leaves a lasting impression and can also get the customer to 'Remark' about their experience to others. I don't need to tell you that word of mouth is still the best form of advertising, and I have always instilled in our staff that the greatest reward for a job well done, is the opportunity to do more work! Now don't get me wrong, this transformation didn't take place overnight. We had plenty of bumps in the road as changing a company culture takes time, but this is what is required to learn and grow. I am proud to say that it has truly been embraced and I'm so proud of our staff for their ability to believe in the concept, and in me!

We implemented weekly surveys for all purchases across all divisions, and as I'm writing this, we have been on a twelve-month streak of 100% satisfaction survey results! As the culture shift continued to develop, we also formulated a new mission statement: "In every encounter and in every interaction, we must leave the world a better place." I wanted to include all aspects of their lives to adhere to the values of 'Professional and Personal Excellence'. Note that we don't strive for perfection, since we are all human beings and that goal is unobtainable. If we put an emphasis on the right attitudes and goal/performance targets, this helps pave the way for achieving them. I ask my staff to write three personal goals in our January staff meeting, so we can follow up during the year-end evaluations to see how they did. I can't express how much each individual has grown, and how many personal goals have been achieved. It is amazing what can be done when you start working together as a team towards one common purpose and find the right people who believe in it as much as you do.

When I came home from the conference the following year, where we won the highest sales growth award, I couldn't wait to call a staff meeting and celebrate with our team. At this time, we still employed the 'Energy Vampire,' and I remember how he shook my hand and said, "Congratulations on your award". WHAT!? This wasn't a personal award; this was a company achievement. I was one of twelve people involved in this and explained that this was a team effort which included him. Everyone was so fired up, but he remained distant. It was another sign that this relationship couldn't continue, as I felt a sense of jealousy and a detachment from the rest of the group. Personal ego has no place in a company. We all have to be in it together or not at all.

I completely changed in terms of management style. I no longer micromanaged our group. I set the standards and expectations, but now allowed individuals to execute the new policies in place. It is amazing what can materialize once you give your employees the opportunity to participate in business decisions. It is absolutely true that the smartest person in the room is the collaboration of everyone in the room! All our divisions were growing, but specifically our flooring division. We were now doing supermarkets, entire schools and other commercial projects that just years earlier I wouldn't have even considered doing, due to lack of ability. We had come together as a team, and the culture was really starting to take hold.

I technically don't have a current fulltime mentor, but Ron would be the closest thing to one for me. We have developed a close relationship throughout the years, and he has always inspired me to challenge myself and my business. Don't get me wrong, everyone in the group has inspired me in some way, John, Kevin, Ryan and the rest of the staff have been extremely influential, but I seem to have a kindred spirit with Ron. A few years ago, he came to see our store in person. This is something he does for all his dealers, another testament to his leadership. We were excited to have him, and I made sure to introduce him to all our staff. He toured our facility and interviewed us to be featured at the next conference. I had a sense of pride when he made mention of us during his opening talk and shared our cultural ideas, as he thought they would be good for others to know and implement. Later that year, I received a message from him asking if I would speak on behalf of the group at a conference of another buying group of which we were a part. He knew I would be attending it. As you might expect from reading this book, I never miss a conference opportunity! He had formed a new alliance with Nationwide, a buying group we are also a part of which included our furniture and appliance products. I was reluctant as I had never spoken publicly before.

It's very different when you're speaking to your staff and your peers compared to a group of strangers! Once again, he indirectly pushed me out of my comfort zone and although I really didn't want to commit, I agreed to do it.

Although the crowd wasn't exactly large, while I was waiting for my introduction, I began feeling quite nervous. I remember saying to myself, "Now look what you've gotten yourself into. You're feeling sick and will probably throw up in front of all of these people." I'm happy to say that once I grabbed the mic, all my sales experience kicked in, and things were fine. I was happy to help my friends!

I was thinking of a new business concept at the time, and although I know that a retail store is essentially its own brand, I was looking to build our very own new mattress brand. But more on that later in the book! I knew the best person I could talk to about business and branding was going to be Ron, and so I asked for a bit of his time, of which he doesn't have much! Ron and I sat down later that evening, had a beer, and I listened to him tell me about his journey in building his own company and brand. Just the fact that he would take time out to talk and be sincerely interested and excited about what I was doing solidified the mentorship relationship. I once again can't express enough how important it is to surround yourself with the right people and taking the time to listen. This is truly how you grow and become a better version of yourself!

Things were going great for our company. We had dug ourselves out of the deep hole we were once in, the staff were embracing our new culture, and sales continued to climb. We had expanded our trade area from what used to be just forty miles, to sixty, and then one hundred. I felt unstoppable and continued with more expansion opportunities and ideas. But as life is full of surprises, we were hearing potentially devastating news. CP Rail, who had been a huge catalyst in our sales growth, was considering changing their business model. They were no longer providing housing in our community, and were even considering shutting down the depot that had been the real reason our town had been constructed in the first place! Knowing people who would have firsthand knowledge of the decision, I contacted them and confirmed our worst fears. They were moving forward with the decision. Our extremely lucrative contract would be coming to an end... Man...F@#k!

IF YOU CAN'T BEAT THEM, JOIN THEM!

Let's take a step back to before I found out the news previously mentioned. I have always followed our current industry trends and was intrigued by the ability to sell our products online. E-commerce was becoming a driving force in the retail business, and I wondered if we should give it a shot. While attending a market for furniture, the tools were now in place to sell products through already developed website managers. We already had our own website but didn't have the knowledge or capability to properly create an e-commerce platform. I visited a group that offered those services and knew that this was going to be the wave of the future. Don't get me wrong, I never considered it to take the place of our current brick and mortar retail store but looked at it as another opportunity to grow sales.

To set the stage, I had recently invited our daughter Chelsey to come back and join the family business. The idea had generated from a Carpets Plus conference I had attended where another business was being featured. The business tugged at my heartstrings as they showed a family company that was part of the group and interviewed the children of the father that had started the business. It is bizarre how emotional these things can get, and I couldn't help but think about how we could possibly bring our kids into the business as the third generation. It probably didn't help that the daughter in the interview was throwing lavish praise upon her father, but nonetheless, the seed was sown!

Angie and I were going on vacation and we were flying out of the city where our daughter was working. She was just about to graduate from college and had been working at a retail store, but not in our industry. She was getting a degree that did not involve business, but had always been part of our company, as any family business would demand. I remember her working with me as a small child, vacuuming carpet rolls and working side by side with Dad! I had the opportunity to stop by the store she was working at and was immediately impressed with how good she was with customers. She never had any desire to return home and work for the family business, but I couldn't help but think that this was a sign. We left the very next day on vacation, but all I could think about was bringing her back to the store.

As soon as we landed after returning home, I called her and explained my plan. Although you don't know me, I can be very persuasive, and I bombarded her with all types of incentives. I would pay off her existing lease, move her back home, offer free rent in an apartment we owned, and on and on! She wasn't sure, but I wouldn't take no for an answer, and before you knew it, she was moving back home. I couldn't have been more excited! Although she had never studied website development or e-commerce, her generation had grown up with this technology. She was also very artistic and creative, so I knew she could help us with this new venture in terms of concepts and ideas. She came to work, and I immediately put her in charge of developing our new website. I was anxious to see how she would perform in sales. After six months, however, it was becoming evident that she wasn't enjoying the stress of being involved in the family business and our retail format just wasn't her passion. She was instrumental in getting us up and running with our first e-commerce website and did a lot of great work, but the day came when she announced that this wasn't for her… Man…F@#k! I knew it too, but I didn't want to admit it. We had a long but good discussion and agreed to part business ways. I am happy that she still lives in our community and seems to have found a good fit for herself professionally. That is the way life goes, and you'll never know unless you try!

We were able to get the website live and active. I chose to develop an entirely different business and website from our own brick and mortar store. Even though the company we hired to facilitate our EDI/API catalog feeds recommended linking it to our store website, I knew that we would be selling for lower margins and didn't want to compete with ourselves. I was so excited and quite proud that we had entered the e-commerce world! We waited with much anticipation for sales to explode. But… nothing happened. I quickly started to learn about SEO and how difficult it was to get the website to have a high ranking online. Finally, after more than a month of being live, our first sale! Here we go, I thought, it won't be long now! Then another two months and… nothing! We had the website active for nine months and had a total of seven sales. At the margins we were selling, the administration fees were taking us into the red. We had a board meeting and decided that this venture wasn't going to work. I called the company I hired and told them to cancel our contract. They replied that they would do it the next day and the dream was lost. Man… F@#k!

I woke up the next morning with an email from the same company, excited to announce that they would be partnering with Amazon. Holy shit, Amazon… Now this was a way to avoid all the digital marketing and SEO concerns! I called them right away and instructed them to cancel our order to shut down and requested a call ASAP to talk about this new opportunity. I received a call later that day and went over the contract details. They explained the terms and conditions, and I immediately signed up. The process to set up a seller account on Amazon wasn't really that brutal but it was something outside of my comfort zone. Again, this is how we learn and grow! It took about a week to complete all the details, but sure enough we would be live on Amazon that same Friday.

My wife and kids were out of town that weekend, so I had the house to myself. I was sitting in the hot tub after work that Friday, when my phone indicated that I had a new email. I opened it up, and there was a seller notification: "Congratulations, you just sold an item on Amazon." I couldn't believe it! We had spent nine months trying to sell items online, and in less than two hours we had sold our first item on Amazon! I remember going to bed that night full of excitement and not really sure what to do next. There was no instruction manual for the process, but nonetheless, I was selling on Amazon! The next morning, I woke up and checked my phone, there were two more emails. "Congratulations, you just sold an item on Amazon!". I immediately called my wife. "We just sold three pieces of furniture on Amazon in less than 24 hours!" We were both excited and once again I was sure I was the smartest man on earth. All day long I received notifications and I think we sold a total of twelve items over the weekend. We had already exceeded the first nine months of sales from our standalone website in just forty eight hours. There would be no stopping us now!

I had an inside rep from Amazon coaching us along the way, but I really had no idea how to manage this new side of the business. We were selling Ashley furniture products as a third-party seller and had to learn all the nuances that came along with placing the orders and getting them shipped to our new customers. I can't reiterate enough that no instruction manual was given as elation quickly turned into stress. We started to learn how to get the business working, but it involved a lot more effort to facilitate the orders. I began working every night, printing the new orders coming in while Angie would place them through our new e-commerce account with Ashley. The work was hard, but the volume of business was incredible. Every time my phone would chirp with a new email, sure enough it was another sale! I started to forecast the volume of sales, and it was clear that we may be selling a million dollars annually. I couldn't have been happier and started to dream about what this could mean for our company, until I dug deeper into the business model.

I had opted to use Fed Ex to ship our products but I wasn't really sure what fees we were paying to get the product delivered. This was never discussed, as many things weren't at the time. So I wasn't sure what exactly the profit margins would be. I knew what I had programed into our markup structure but had no way of looking up what the shipping costs were. I contacted all the parties that were involved, and nobody could give me an answer. I spent nearly an hour on the phone with Fed Ex trying to find out why I didn't have individual billing statements and was told I would just have to wait until we received our monthly statements. I finally got somebody to give me an idea of what we were paying for a common item being sold, and they informed me that since it was oversized, it would be around $120. What! We were only making around $40 profit on this item, so here we were losing $80 on every sale! No wonder business was great, I was the lowest price in the world! Our elation quickly turned to devastation and fear. Remember, this was after nearly three weeks of high-volume sales, totaling close to $40,000. Man...F@#k!

Another wonderful development taking place was that we quickly learned about performance metrics on Amazon. You have to give delivery expectations to your customers. The faster you ship, the higher you rank! But if you are late on your shipping promises, you get a negative performance metric rating. If you want to add insult to injury, we were now learning that the API/EDI feeds we were working with were unreliable. This meant that the amount of inventory available being reported at the factory was inaccurate, so many of the orders placed would be backordered. This puts your account at risk of being shut down as a seller if you exceed their high-performance metric demands. Here we were just getting started and already we were being threatened to shut down, as well as losing money! There was no way to know which items were considered oversized and which were not, and we were suddenly frantic to figure this out. Our online customers were getting the best deal in the land, Amazon was making their cut, Ashley was selling tons of products through us, and the company facilitating the inventory feed was making their fees. Only we were doing all the work, and potentially losing our ass!

Needless to say, after just a few months I figured I might not be the smartest guy on the planet after all. I made call after call to all the parties involved but couldn't get any answers. I found some solutions by adding additional warehouse locations to ship from to avoid backorder issues, but this required setting up sales tax permits in eleven states across the country. As you might guess, this also meant spending more money and legal fees. As Vince Lombardi has been quoted, "What the hell is going on out here!" Man…F@#k!

We finally stabilized some of the issues by identifying which items were oversized, but really with no help from anybody. It is amazing and disappointing that details are not divulged in your startup agreement. Here I was working harder than ever before in my life and I was losing money… Man…F@#k! I was so pissed off at Fed Ex for not providing me with the information I needed that we switched our shipping contract to UPS, although they really don't have that much of a different policy. We proceeded with the expansion of distribution centers to clean up our performance metrics and continue to sell Ashley on Amazon today. We have finally made it profitable, but it remains a challenging business model!

So there we were, now that our main company was finally doing well for itself, I found us subsidizing the losses from our e-commerce division. We were burning through cash once again, and I couldn't help but think that we were headed back to the same place we had been so many years before. With the loss of our CP Rail contract, we no longer had the cushion we once enjoyed... What was I going to do? Man...F@#k!

BY THE POWER OF
THE HOLY SPIRIT

I went to bed one night still stressed with all the concerns we had moving forward on Amazon. I knew this was the way of the future for retail, but could we make any money doing it? I had also been reading about this new business in the mattress industry called "beds-in-a-box" and I was intrigued about this new delivery method. Major brands like Tuft and Needle, Casper, and Ghost were really starting to see success with it. In the year 2012, I think the industry had done around a little over twenty million dollars but were now projecting sales in the hundreds of millions. I had the opportunity to sell the same brands that I sold out of my retail store online, as everyone was beginning to enter this market. I remember thinking from my Ashley experience, "How can I make money selling the same products as everyone else, when everyone is driving prices and profits to the bottom?" I was exhausted and finally fell asleep; however, there was plenty on my mind.

I woke up that same morning around 3:30 am and almost sprung out of bed. I've got it! I'll design my own mattress and brand! I'll make it different and better than what is currently out there… and by the power of the Holy Spirit… I'll make this happen! I couldn't even fall back to sleep. Again, not to bring religion into the equation, but this wasn't the first time I felt providence at work. I started typing an email to myself and I instantly thought of a name. I would call this new company and product, Cloud 9 Sleep! I was so excited to share this with my wife and family. We had a brief discussion about the idea over breakfast, and everyone agreed that it was pretty cool. However, I don't think anybody believed that this was going to happen. How could it happen? We can't manufacturer mattresses! I decided to reach out to a local plant from where we were sourcing other brands to see if they were interested in building my new product and brand. I called the manufacturing plant that sourced our existing brands that very same morning, and much to my surprise, they were interested in my idea. Since I knew my kids were more tech-savvy, I had them go online and find a trademark company to secure our new Cloud 9 Sleep brand. I gave them my credit card to secure the mark and we were on our way! It didn't take long after researching the trademark status that there were already hundreds of companies using that very same name. Here we go again, I just spent money on something that wouldn't come to fruition, what the hell was I doing... Man...F@#k!

I decided to move forward regardless. The worst-case scenario would be a name change. There was just something about the prompting I had that felt like this was the right thing to do! I made an appointment to visit the plant and started to design our new product. When I arrived at the plant, I was pleasantly surprised that they had some ideas for me. I had never designed a product in my life and I wasn't well-versed in manufacturing mattresses. They had a lot of foundational ideas, since they were already building products for other brands in the "bed-in-a-box" industry. I was informed about the high compression rate these mattresses would be put under, and the need for the right materials required to get them to rebound. As we looked at all the construction options we could build with, I was intrigued by a new product called 'copper-infused latex.' Though we would not be the first to introduce this to the market, I quickly realized that nobody was really putting an emphasis on it. This was during a period when copper products were really catching wind, like copper body wraps, apparel, cookware, bracelets, etc. I had known many people in my local community who swore by the healing benefits of copper and I saw a unique market opportunity.

After a few hours of trial and error, I felt good about the design of three firmness models we would build. I agreed to have the prototypes made and couldn't wait for them to be built and shipped out for testing. Now came the new struggle of what we would call the new brand, since our original name was not going to work. After much debate and thought, we came up with CopperRest Sleep. We designed a logo and hired a law firm that specialized in filing for trademarks - I wouldn't make the same mistake twice!

The next hurdle would be to contact Amazon and set up a second seller account. This wasn't usually allowed, but we were able to get the account approved and called our new seller account CopperRest Sleep. Unlike our Ashely seller account which had been built and designed for us by a third party, I would be on my own when it came to creating item listings for our new products and the creation of a new website. This would involve hiring a professional photographer and learning all kinds of new jargon with regards to the internet and Amazon requirements. You don't just turn on a switch and go! I had nobody on staff that had any knowledge of these things and I was not going to spend more money to get it done. So, with the help of my Amazon representative, I quickly put on another hat and became our IT guy! Tons and tons of late nights lay ahead, as it's difficult to focus on these things during regular business hours. You may have forgotten, but I was still running a pretty busy retail store. Keep in mind that our other Ashley Amazon account was still going bat-shit crazy, so I was putting those fires out and dealing with very high-volume sales.

Then, in my free time, I would learn about and build our new mattress listings, plus we had decided to make this an FBA account.

There are two ways to sell retail on Amazon. One is fulfilled by merchant (FBM) and the other is fulfilled by Amazon (FBA). With FBM you are a third-party seller. A customer orders the product you list, and it's up to you to ship it to the customer and get it delivered. You have no inventory in any of Amazon's distribution centers. With FBA, you physically ship your products to wherever Amazon chooses, to any of their multiple distribution centers across the country. You have money invested in stocking their warehouses and pay storage fees for the space. The advantage is that it immediately qualifies you for prime shipping status and increases your profile rank. Amazon then takes care of all the shipping and tracking, so you basically watch orders come through and wait to get paid. This sounded a hell of a lot better than what I was doing with the Ashley account. And, since this was my own brand, I could make money when I sold these items, as I knew all the manufacturing and shipping costs. This was all taking time however, and once the prototypes were accepted, we wouldn't activate our seller account to go live for over three more months. Another long trial, but hopefully the effort would pay off.

Hey, let's go see how the trademark is coming along. This was also important, since having a trademark serial number on Amazon propelled you into a higher listing status. This wasn't only about intellectual property rights, this would help with marketing and sales. So, let's go check in with our attorneys and see how things are going...

I had the ability to monitor the status of our trademark online directly with the government website, but I didn't see much activity. We had the trademark filed at this point for over three months. I was beginning to learn the policy, procedure and glacial speed at which the government works! We had done a basic word search for the CopperRest trademark, and the attorney working our case felt pretty confident that it would go through. It was just a matter of time. I asked them to keep me informed and I was anxious to get it done. I had in the meantime been selling the CopperRest mattress products in my retail store and was getting plenty of great feedback from our customers. I obviously couldn't wait to get the "beds-in-a-box" items live on Amazon. But something kept bothering me in the back of my mind... What if we don't get the trademark? What would we do and what would that mean? I started checking the trademark website daily, sometimes two, three times a day. I just really needed this to get done!

Meanwhile, we chose January 1st to be the launch day of our Amazon account for CopperRest Sleep, "The World's Healthiest Mattress". As the day approached, all of the hard work in creating the photos and images, bullet-point information on the listings, setting up UPC codes for the products, and of course getting a bunch of inventory shipped and checked into a multitude of Amazon distribution centers, was going to pay off. I remember right after Christmas that year, I almost couldn't contain the excitement of our launch. With the high volume of sales we were experiencing on the other account, though at low profit, here was our chance to have that same volume, but now at margins that would make us more profitable than we could imagine. This would help take the place of the loss of business we had experienced from CP Railroad and truly set us up for the future!

Finally, it arrived... January 1st, the launch date! I got confirmation from our representative that things were turned on and I confirmed it by going onto Amazon's website. Sure enough, there was our new brand and its products! It was a pretty awesome feeling. This wasn't somebody else's product that we were selling online, this was our own personal design, brand name, and logo. Nobody but us had this product available for sale, and I am not being arrogant, but we had developed a really great mattress. Now I couldn't wait to get the rest of the USA to give it a try.

See, that's the thing that gets overlooked about e-commerce. As much of a headache as it had been at the beginning, in our first year selling Ashley on Amazon we shipped over 1200 pieces of furniture to literally every state in the lower forty eight states! Here was this small-town retailer selling nationally. Now was the opportunity for us to take our very own brand nationally. That is why I continued to stick it out and negotiate our way through the process. Instead of expanding our trade area by hundreds of miles, we expanded by thousands of miles, all with the click of a button!

The instant we went live, I was like an online stalker in terms of my own account dashboard! I would check if there were sales every fifteen minutes. I checked all day and all night long, but nothing... Oh well, I thought, I'll go to bed and check in the morning. See, it wasn't uncommon at all to wake up and have several seller sales notifications. Online customers have strange shopping hours! I woke up the next morning and didn't do a thing but head for the computer to check our account. Nothing? Weeks passed... nothing. What was going on? I had all this money invested in infrastructure, time, and inventory. My other Ashley account was still going crazy, so it wasn't a sales slump. What was going on? Man... F@#k!

My Amazon representative had taken some time off during the launch, so it was a week before I could get in touch with him to discuss my disappointment. As you might expect, I was pretty anxious to have a conversation, as my expectations were grossly missed! As he began to respond to my concerns, once again it was evident that somebody should provide a manual for doing business online. Don't get me wrong, Amazon has tons of video tutorials, almost too many, but they are so specific. I think just the simple broad strokes of how things work would be a great idea. As I listened, I began to learn more and more about listing ranking on Amazon. See, Ashely was being sold long before we came along, so from all the time, sales volume, customer reviews, and so on, those listings ranked extremely high. As a result, I had never spent one penny on advertising on Amazon, which of course they are happy to provide to you for a fee! I didn't need to spend any money, because Ashley was already such a well-established brand and product listing. I soon discovered that getting the first sale of a new brand that nobody knew about and getting my first review would be paramount to picking up the sales momentum. The best way to do this was to set up an advertising campaign on Amazon. I would need to invest a substantial amount of money to see results. Man…F@#k!

Becoming more obsessed, I checked our account every five minutes it seemed. I was still taking care of other business, but any chance I had, I was looking at our seller dashboard. Now, instead of seeing sales, I was watching our account balance go into the red due to the money we were spending on advertising. How could I have missed this goal and target by so much?

Finally, our first sale. It took almost a month from the launch date, but it was still pretty exciting. Here was a king-size mattress, shipping all the way to Hawaii in a box 20"x20"x40"! Not to mention, it was our design and brand. I couldn't wait to see how the customer liked it. But new anxieties kicked in. Would the shipping process work? What if there was damage? What if the bed didn't rebound as it should? Even worse, what if they didn't like it! Days passed with no new sales, but then a spark of hope as the first customer left us our first review, and it was glowing! I remember the sense of pride we all had, not because of what we had achieved financially, but from the simple affirmation of customer satisfaction. That was still the primary goal, exceeding the customer's expectations and leaving the world a better place than we found it! We were excited to have our customer sleeping well.

Sales slowly started to come in, and for the first quarter we averaged about four sales per month. Nothing exciting, but progress, however not anywhere near what I was expecting. This was starting to weigh on my mind, because at this volume, we could not be profitable. I knew from experience that most businesses take up to three years before they turn a profit. Hell, most of the major brand names in the industry doing hundreds of millions in sales, are still not making a profit. But I had a simple and small business model. If we could do ten units a month, I could breakeven. How could we get to this level... Oh yeah, the trademark will help! Let's check in on that progress again.

As I was checking our Amazon dashboard every free chance I got, I was checking the trademark website. I decided to check it one more time before I called our attorney's office. We were supposed to get approval no later than six months after filing the application and we were on the final week of that six-month period. As I mentioned before, the government moves at glacial speed! If they say up to six months, it will be six months! As I checked on the current status, I was blown away that there had been some updates. I picked up the phone with excitement and contacted our attorney's office. She began telling me she would email me the correspondence, but it was "Not exactly the news we were hoping for." "What does that mean?" I asked. "Well, they found some other conflicts and have denied the mark at this time." It felt like all the blood had drained out of my body as I began to sweat and panic. After all this time and a second trademark application, not to mention the costs of filing them, I couldn't protect my product and brand, which I had been selling locally for six months and nationally for three! She proceeded to tell me that we could file an appeal and there was a good chance that they could argue against the objections, and that the trademark should still go through. Well, alright then, let's go! It was too late to turn back as we were actively doing business. I hung up the phone and verbally said out loud, "Man...F@#k!"

Here came that old feeling again... Maybe I was fooling myself. I have no education and I had entered into something that seemed doomed to fail. How could God call me to this and then not want me to succeed? Unfortunately, there were plenty more challenges on the horizon...

MI FAMILIA

Sorry to take a break from the drama, but I thought I would take some time to introduce my family. You may have noticed a little Spanish in the title of this chapter, but let me inform you that the only other words I know are, *Dos cerveza's, por favor*!

My wife and I both come from larger families. I only have two sisters and Angie has four, but my parents both came from a family of seven, so family was important growing up. It's also worth mentioning, because throughout a lot of the struggles and successes, our families were a big part of our support. As you read earlier, my wife was my first official hire. She did such a great job, I had to marry her! That way she could never leave... Haha! (She probably feels that way). We had been junior high sweethearts growing up, but lost touch a bit during high school, as I was away a lot playing music. So, when she moved back to Harvey and agreed to come and work for us, there was still a bit of the old spark! She is a beautiful lady inside and out, so sometimes she was a distraction at work. We were married a few years later, and both had children prior, so we began our blended family. Our three oldest daughters in order are Kirsché, Chelsey and Aubrey. Soon after marriage, we were pregnant with our twins Quincy and Spencer. Why do we use the expression "we" were pregnant? Nothing happened to me!

It was always a busy household, so with both of us working, including during the bad times, it was amazing that we were able to keep things together. We kept a lot of the struggles hidden away from our children, but it wasn't always possible. Like any family business, the kids were always involved, even to the slightest degree, as they would spend time with us after school, and even when we worked late. The twins, however, got the same treatment that I got from my father - involuntary work orders! Since there were two of them, it was a perfect combination for delivery, warehouse work, floorcovering installation, and so on. Even though they did enjoy growing up in the business, the work they helped with wasn't necessarily easy, so work began early in the morning, which was not an ideal situation during their high school years. But they always did a good job and kept a good attitude. To me, experience is still the best way to learn.

As was mentioned previously, after my spiritual retreat, our marriage was really rekindled. As a result, we had two more children. Boys again, Christopher and Matthew. As I'm writing this, Chris will soon be ten-years old, and Matt is eight. They haven't got quite enough meat on their bones to do the hard work, but little do they know, it's coming! They have been actively involved in the business however, because we talk all the time about how the business is going. Like their older siblings they spend at the business after school, and they have even helped with a new mattress design. Actually, they inspired it! I still have the product development drawing they made for me one night when I was working late. We'll get into that story later.

I talk a lot about my parents, as I should in terms of founding the business, but through much of the years we owned the store, Angie's parents were a big part of what we achieved in terms of spiritual support. I always admired Angie's parents. For most of the time I had known them (remember I frequented their place a lot during junior high) they had always been so joyful. Not that my parents weren't, but the stresses of the business would come through in my household growing up. So, when I experienced such a dynamically different level of peace, it was hard not to feel it. Things would later change for Leo and Ruth, but during the early parts of our marriage, they didn't have much in what society would call wealth. They had a nice home and cars, but nothing extravagant. They didn't travel on vacation or go on trips but they were always so content and happy. This always seemed strange to me, since my parents seemed to have all of what society would consider successful, and yet they never seemed content. A significant part of Leo and Ruth's happiness was their faith. Even before my journey began, they had already planted the seeds. I remember how easy it was to talk to them, especially to Leo in terms of a father-in-law. Going through my struggles, it was hard to talk about the business challenges with my own father, since they would directly affect him. So, during some of my lowest emotional points, it was good to have the support I had from my father-in-law. Leo passed away in 2016 after a battle with cancer. He was a great man in terms of what he gave back to everyone who knew him. He was also a big inspiration for our new mission statement, and my son Spencer has drafted up bylaws for a new non-profit group that we intend to found in his name. The Leo R. Rutten Foundation will continue to be an instrument in his honor, helping those in need, wherever it is needed.

Our oldest daughter Kirsché is married and has given us three grandchildren. Our second daughter Chelsey graduated with a classical arts degree and is currently in the banking industry. Our third daughter Aubrey graduated with a teaching degree and is actively teaching. My sons Quincy and Spencer will both graduate with business and finance degrees and I'm excited to say, will return to the family business. My excitement stems first and foremost from the fact that, as you've been reading, I really could use the help! The future is still uncertain for our youngest, Chris and Matt, but just like all my other children, I'm sure they'll turn out perfectly. I haven't been the best father or husband by any means, but I have always tried to be honest and fair. I have encouraged my kids that they can be anything they set their minds to. Believe it to achieve it and Be Remarkable Today! "Blessed is the man whose quiver is full."

Now, don't get me wrong, it wasn't always stress and conflict with my own family. My parents were very supportive of what I did, but they didn't always express it. In junior high I won first place in the wrestling tournament. This also gave me an opportunity to qualify for state as I was a pretty small kid, so I wrestled the lightest weight class. I came home with my trophy and was excited to tell my dad what I had achieved. When he saw the trophy, he asked if everyone in the tournament had laid down for me! This wasn't a dig to be mean - that was just the way he expressed his emotions by trying to be funny. I had another achievement in high school when I won the Science Olympiad Tournament for electronics. When I presented the gold medal, he replied, "Was this the Special Olympics Tournament?" Again, it wasn't that he wasn't proud of me, that is simply how we communicated. We are a fun family and giving each other shit is kind of how we roll!

My parents conceived me when my mother was only sixteen. In those days, that meant getting married. I'm happy to say that as I'm writing this, they are about to celebrate their 50th wedding anniversary. When my parents got married at such a young age, my father decided to join the Navy. He knew that he needed to support my mother and me, and there wasn't much opportunity in our town. So, he went off to basic training and my mother and I stayed at my grandparents' home. My grandfather was an extremely hardworking man. He farmed and worked for a small grain elevator company. I remember the many summers I would stay with them. It's weird how the physical sensations stay with you, as I can still feel, smell and hear the sights and sounds of the farm. My grandmother was hardworking and relatively strict. They had seven children in a three-bedroom farmhouse! They didn't have much for most of their lives, but it never seemed like it. Unfortunately, they lost two children to automobile accidents and being a father myself now, I have no idea how they got through the experience. I learned so much from them and with plenty of aunts, uncles, and cousins, we always did things together... Family was everything!

My father has always been my hero and excelled in the Navy. He quickly moved up in rank and received many achievement awards. I remember asking a question one night soon after the horrible financial discovery after the fire. I was revealing, with terrible shame, what the status of the business was and asking for some advice on what he might do. It was very emotional because I figured in just less than two years, I was about to take down something that had taken him nearly 20 years to build up from nothing. I remember feeling so low and asked why he had even considered my ultimatum and sold the business to me. He should just said, "See ya!" and booted my ass out the door. His response pops up in my head almost every day. He said, "I sold it to you because I knew you would run it better." Was he crazy, especially to say that at that particular moment? To me, that is the greatest example of leadership I have ever witnessed in my life. Here was a man who had built a company from scratch and who was willing to walk away, still in his prime, because he saw a better future for the business in me! It was truly one of the most humbling moments of my life, and all of the missed accolades of the past were erased... It was the first time in a long time that my father hugged me and told me that he loved me.

I couldn't possibly write this book and not include my mother.

We have always had a great relationship. Since I already explained that our whole family is kind of crazy, it seems to be my mission in life to pick on my mom. Not to intentionally make her mad but giving each other shit is just how we roll! But her story is inspiring. To start, there was the decision to have me! That was an incredible decision for such a young woman. Secondly, being the wife of a sailor! My dad would be out to sea for long periods of time, and that left her raising me and my sister, Cherie, alone. Then when we moved back to start the store, like all small family businesses, it was all hands on deck! She would work all day and take care of the household as well. My mom is quite short and small. I joke with her all the time that she should technically have to ride in a car seat! She'll be pissed when she reads this, but she is probably expecting it! She was only 90 pounds for most of the time we were running the store. I mention this because she could physically out-work any man we ever had at our store throughout the years. She had the gift of the gab and she is very easy to talk to - which is the foundation of a great salesperson. While my dad took care of the service and business decisions, she was a big part of what made us grow in terms of sales. She has battled cancer three times and won, so she is also a woman you don't want to mess with! She was put in the middle of many arguments between my father and I, and is still a great sounding board to this day. She truly is a woman to admire!

WE WON'T BE
FOOLED AGAIN...

So, back to the action! For a moment, I thought we were back on track for the trademark. A simple appeal and argument should clear things up, but this would take another three months to accomplish. I would have to figure out other ways to stimulate growth in terms of sales on Amazon. There were some positive signs: sales in the second quarter were climbing to seven a month, pretty close to the breakeven point. Even more exciting were all the positive reviews! This is probably what kept me sane during this time, because if nobody liked the product, I would have just stopped the venture. Quite the contrary though, everyone loved our product, and I would even get phone calls from customers telling me personally how much they loved their new mattress. We were hearing the same thing locally, so I knew this was something that had to be pursued. There must be a way to succeed... Where's my damn manual? Man...F@#k!

I got an email from our attorney's office to say that the lawyer in charge of my trademark case had been let go from the firm. What did this mean and what happens next? The email was from one of the partners of the firm who asked when was a good time to talk on the phone. RIGHT NOW would probably be a good time to talk! So, I replied that I was available for an immediate phone call.

He began to advise me that the previous attorney had been a little loose and unthorough in her research and filing an appeal would probably be a losing effort. If he would have reviewed our case, he would not have advised us to apply for a CopperRest Sleep trademark application. He would be happy to file the appeal, but it would take three more months, and most likely be denied. Man...F@#k! Now what do I do? I couldn't make a name change and start over. I had been selling products all over the country by now, not to mention I had spent over $30,000 just on Amazon for brand awareness. I couldn't just scratch the whole idea and concept! What about protection of our intellectual property? Could somebody out there order a cease and desist action against us? I had no idea what to do. I told him I would discuss the options with our group and get back to him on how to proceed.

I don't think I slept for more than an hour that night. I talked mainly to Angie and the twins, but it really was more of a venting session. I was completely deflated and quickly losing the confidence and spirit to go on. For a couple of months, as I had been trying to formulate a strategy that would help grow sales, price had come up as a possible reason for low sales. Our CopperRest mattresses were a premium product and not just another memory foam bed. When we began researching, designing and manufacturing mattresses, I failed to mention that I had considered options other than just the original plant. I had discovered that at the time, around 90% of all "beds-in-a-box" were imported from primarily the same two manufacturers in China. What I had the option of doing was selecting from already designed mattresses and putting my own private label them. So, you could create a brand, but not a product. There was also no control over quality and health concerns, and they were on the proverbial "slow boat from China." It disappointed me that this was what most of the major competing brands were doing at the time, so although we had price quotes, we chose to go our own way. Because we were so committed to creating something new and something significantly better, this increased production costs. But for the quality of the product, it was still tremendous value, we just needed to grow and get the word out. While reflecting on all of this, I had considered that maybe I should design something for a little less money and eliminating the copper technology would lower the costs. I hadn't wanted to start over with a new brand, trademark, etc., but now I was faced with that very choice. Maybe a new parent brand name could be the new trademark, and I could develop new products and series as the brand expanded... Hey, we might be on to something! Like most challenges I face, these are the thoughts going through my head at 4:00 am, but that is how I process. I keep working on the problem in my mind, and hopefully a solution develops. This might be the solution to our problems, but it would require a new capital investment to develop new products, new inventory, and even more legal fees. I decided I'd call our attorneys the next day.

I called first thing in the morning with our new idea, but this time insisted on vetting the trademark option to the point of certainty before filing. We won't be fooled again! Now came the process of thinking of a new name that would apply and encompass what our brand and products were all about. With the collaboration of their team and ours, we finally decided on Accord Comfort Sleep Systems, "Providing You Peace of Mind, Body and Spirit." We were advised that since we had been doing business already as CopperRest Sleep, if awarded the new parent brand trademark, protection for all other products and series names would be included under this umbrella as well. The main partner of the legal firm felt this name would be a solid chance, so we scrapped the appeal and moved forward with a new trademark name and application. The only catch was it started the process all over again. The trademark office posted, "Applications can take up to six months to process," and as I mentioned earlier, that meant six months... Man...F@#k!

This also meant that it was time to develop new products! Wanting to keep the quality, but help lower the costs, we removed the copper infused gel/latex layers and some of the body comfort layers. This simply resulted in a slightly firmer feel and change in overall size. We are incredibly proud of our 8" base and support core and have a patent pending on what we refer to as our "Accord Comfort Reflex Layer." I won't bore you with all the technical details (you can check out the website – www.accordsleep.com) but I was adamant in keeping this consistent in all our mattress lineups. That way the internal quality and support remains the same, and the only change in price is size and body comfort technology. Hence the introduction of our 8" Whisper Breeze and our 10" Gentle Night mattresses.

After design, we had to build the prototypes, work out any bugs, and even scarier, build new listings on Amazon, get professional photos and image files, build new bullet point listings, register new UPC codes, build and send more inventory into Amazon, and worse still… I had built our active e-commerce website for CopperRest Sleep. This would no longer be the only product and brand name - it was now obsolete. I would have to build another website as well… Man…F@#k!

I had hired Angie's sister Mary to help us with our CopperRest website in terms of SEO and other digital marketing aspects. She had been doing this for another company, and I trusted her abilities as they were superior to mine. She agreed to be subcontracted and did a great job on improving our online indexing. Sales were starting to pick up but remained inconsistent. We had months that now surpassed breakeven, but it seemed all the profit we made would simply be reinvested in marketing and capital expenses. Now with the need for a new website, all the work she did for us would be lost. What the hell was I doing? I really didn't have the additional capital to invest in this new restructure, so now we were starting to set up new loans and lines of credit and going further into debt! Keep in mind that most of our major competitors were venture capital groups, so we were playing in a field that had more financial resources than we did. The drive kept coming from more and more satisfied customers and the belief in our product, but could I get through starting up from scratch again? I decided that this time, I would need some help as I would soon run out of support from our Amazon representative.

When you set up your seller account on Amazon, you only get one year of support and that timeline was on the horizon. I would have to act quickly, as I couldn't retain all the knowledge of creating new listings. I asked Mary if she knew anyone that could help. She was working full time and couldn't commit to the time that would be required to help us. She put me in touch with a guy that had experience in the digital marketing field and arranged a meeting. I met with them both and decided that I liked what I heard and signed a contract with him to help with photos, image files, building the listings, and eventually marketing. As you would expect, this was another new capital expense, but if you are going to play with the big boys, you have to do big things. We had to work quickly as I only had a few months left with Amazon support. To his credit he did fulfil his contract obligations but had never built listings on Amazon before, so he had to learn on the job with the help of our rep. To my relief, it wasn't me doing all the work. I never could fully remove myself from running our retail business, so I was definitely starting to burn out. To my staff's credit, they were embracing our cultural change so well, that they were making it easier for me to run the company. It didn't change the fact that there were still plenty of late nights and there was still the website issue. If you have never been in the digital world, it is amazing the fees everybody demands to do this kind of work. We had price quotes on building a new site, but I just couldn't accept paying the costs they were asking, so I took on the task of building a new one myself. Also, it was time to build the new products and get them into inventory in Amazon. The new trademark application had been sent, and to our law firm's credit, they agreed to do it at no additional charge. I was pleasantly surprised during a whirlwind of chaos... Man…F@#k!

FAILURE TO LAUNCH

There were some logistical issues starting to rear their ugly heads in terms of our current manufacturing relationship. Now I have to be clear here, I couldn't have been working with a better team of people. The owner of the plant was as good of a man as you will find, however, they did not have the equipment to roll pack our mattresses. This meant they would build them, but then ship them to another location two states away to be roll packed. Originally, this entire process was supposed to take seven to ten days, but as we began selling more products and we needed to replenish inventory in Amazon, the turnaround time was taking two to three weeks. In the online world, if you don't have product available, the customer is going to move on and make another purchase elsewhere, so this was becoming a concern. I suggested that they invest in a roll packing machine, but they weren't willing to make the commitment. I don't blame them, a quality machine could easily run north of $300,000! As crazy as this sounds, I actually considered the investment. This would also mean I would have to build a new distribution warehouse, since we were completely at full warehouse capacity in our retail store. I looked into lease financing, but at the end of the day, we simply didn't have the sales to justify such a large investment - it would have been financial suicide. Unfortunately, it was becoming clear that if we were going to do this and meet our projected goals, our current manufacturing relationship wasn't going to work. I would have to consider looking elsewhere and yet I loved the people I was working with. They taught and helped me so much in terms of industry knowledge and design, it didn't seem fair… Man…F@#k!

All my concerns were made crystal clear on the initial order to get the new products into Amazon. It was a very large order and another major investment for us. We had worked hard to get all the infrastructure done in terms of listings and we were now waiting for the product to arrive at Amazon. For some reason, this order was the most delayed and we ended up with damage during roll packing. This required sending the damaged product back to the plant, having it rebuilt and shipping it again to be roll packed. All in all, it took over thirty days to complete this order. This was unacceptable, though it wasn't intentional, and something would have to change. We were experiencing a failure to launch! I started to research other manufacturers, and to my dismay, they were mostly similar to the importing guys. They wouldn't make our beds to specifications; they would simply put our brand and label on products they had already designed. This wasn't even an option. Our design was the key to our success, so I was feeling trapped. I decided to reach out to a guy I had spoken to months before about digital marketing ideas, since we still weren't moving forward as quickly as I would have liked. Bill was affiliated with the group that facilitated our Ashely Amazon seller account, and I was really just interested in seeing if he had any marketing ideas. Amazingly, once I described what we were going through, he put me in touch with another person who was representing a plant that was building for other "bed-in-a-box" retailers. They were located in Chicago and he thought we should talk. He made the introduction with James at the plant, and I was happy to hear that they were willing to build our beds to specifications. Now the long process of traveling to this new plant and starting over with prototypes to ensure the design would be the same.

I had built a new website that was basically just about product knowledge. I had given up on making the website active in terms of e-commerce and when Bill looked at it, he asked why there wasn't e-commerce? I explained that the bulk of our sales were coming from our Amazon platform. Bill is a brutally honest guy, so he quickly challenged me on the decision and told me my website design was crap! You might be thinking I was offended. Even though I didn't think the site was crap, I really appreciated his honesty. We discussed what it would cost him to build a new site and his price was fairly reasonable compared to other quotes I had received in the past. But here we went again, spending more money and bleeding cash. It reminded me of a book I read where an analogy was given entitled, *The Messy Middle*. The analogy describes deciding to swim across the English Channel. You prepare and work for the opportunity. You have your goal set and envision your success. You take off from one shoreline and things are going really well. You are full of confidence and feel like nothing can stop you. However, you get to the halfway point and fatigue sets in. You began to lose steam and start treading water. You look back and realize that you're halfway there, but now uncertain if you can make it the rest of the way. You begin to question what you were even thinking in the first place, "I'm going to drown out here!" You realize that going back is just as far as going forward, and if you turn back you would have failed on your dream. So, you find your second wind and start moving forward again towards your goal. This was precisely where I was at, either I go back and fail, drown, or get my ass to work and finish the race!

I agreed to Bill's contract and he immediately got to work on the site. I literally had design templates forwarded to me within forty-eight hours. I liked his aggressive style and he didn't mess around in terms of time. When he said he was going to do something, he did it. Reminiscent to what my father had taught me as a young man. In just a couple of weeks, the site was built and exceeded my expectations. Even though the work was more involved that he thought, he held true to his contract and not a penny more... Nice!

Meanwhile, at the Bat Cave... Sorry, I'm a nerd, remember! It was time for me to make a trip to Chicago. We did get the initial order to Amazon for the new products, but much to my dismay, the lower prices weren't the catalyst we expected to increase sales. If anything, it helped us sell more of our CopperRest series. I met with James and Ed, the owner of the plant. Like before, we went into the design room where they had all the raw materials to our specifications so I could confirm the design was correct. We instantly hit it off, as they were a family owned business just like us. Ed has his kids and wife involved in operations, so this felt very familiar to me. I toured the plant, and it was exactly what we needed. They had three roll packing machines and massive production and warehouse capacity! We had already negotiated a price, which of course was less than what we were paying simply due to all phases being done in one location. Everything seemed to be in order, and we agreed to the new partnership. I remember finally feeling a sense of relief, even though money kept pouring out from this venture. I was making my way past the "messy middle" but, man, I was fatigued... Man...F@#k!

THE CALL

We had been investing so much money in new inventory, marketing costs, website development and this list goes on, that I was beginning to max out our lines of credit. It was time to go to the bank and refinance the business. I remember sitting in the meeting with our lender explaining what was taking place and selling our business plan. To our banker's credit, he was skeptical of what we were doing and if it should continue. We had finally built up the equity to borrow the money for our e-commerce ventures, but to date hadn't made any money. Frankly, we were losing money! He was more than willing to make the new loans but cautioned us whether this was the right thing to do. It's hard to convey your dream to others sometimes, especially when it's such an unfamiliar business model. Being in a small town, the goals we had set rarely happened in a community like ours. It was an uncomfortable meeting, but we proceeded with the new loans and bought ourselves a little breathing room.

Our online business was still growing, but not at the pace we would have liked. During this time, a new idea had set in. Perhaps we should set up wholesale distribution and establish other dealers to help generate consistent volume and profit, even if it would be at slimmer margins? With the help of our new manufacturing partners, we decided that providing a small showroom footprint displaying our products and holding the in-stock inventory still in a box would be the best format. That way we could target retailers that were either not in the mattress business or had limited showroom capacity. This would also create an opportunity for a more cash and carry business model, not requiring as much warehouse space or delivery. I believed that this concept would be a great idea, but how would I get it implemented and find qualified dealers? This would now require the development of a new carton in which to package our products, as we had just been delivering our online sales in a manila box with a sticker of our logo - not what you would expect on a retail showroom floor. We came up with a beautiful design, but it would require another $8,000 investment just to create the dye and casting for the box... Man...F@#k! Then we got the call.

I was sitting in my office when the phone rang, and I got a page: "Rod line two." Now, we have four active phone lines, but line two is either directed at our service department or is piggybacked to our tollfree number. For some reason, most telemarketer calls come to me on this line. I pick up the phone and a woman proceeded to introduce herself as representing Kevin Harrington, an original Shark from Shark Tank. I already knew that this was a telemarking call. I let her finish her pitch, as she explained how their company, which works with Kevin and his AsSeenOnTv company, was interested in our Accord Comfort Sleep Systems products. She would like to establish a follow-up call and was excited to work with us on our mattresses. RIGHT... I indulged her on the pitch and agreed to the follow-up call. I challenged her as to how she even knew about our company, we weren't doing anything substantial yet, and she explained that they were always looking for new product ideas, came across our website and thought we might be a good fit. Now to be fair, after the phone call, I didn't know if she was asking us to be on Shark Tank or what was really happening. I was very skeptical and was ready to dismiss the call as simply another telemarketer.

She sent me a follow-up email explaining that I would be getting calls from other members of their organization. Included in the email were the names of the people involved in the process. I immediately turned to Google, since I had never expected an email in the first place. I started to research the company and names involved with the organization. I was now getting a little spooked as things began to appear legitimate. I informed Angie, Quincy and Spencer, who at the time were still in college. I asked them to vet the organization because there had to be some catch... This was too good to be true! No offense to Kevin, but I never really watched Shark Tank, so I didn't know who he was. It didn't take long to discover that he was a successful entrepreneur and really did represent the companies in the pitch. But what was the catch, this didn't feel right? Why would anyone with so much success be willing to talk to a company like ours? The twins had done their homework and confirmed that all the people involved in the organization were who they said they were. The introductions were made via email, and the follow-up call came.

The next call explained what they were offering. They were offering a celebrity endorsement from Kevin Harrington and they were going to list our products on the AsSeenOnTv.pro website. They would include three hundred sixty-second commercial spots on national cable networks in the markets of our choice... Aha... this was a solicitation after all! This could be ours for the low price of $25,000! My suspicion was confirmed - this was just another telemarking call! I agreed to the next follow-up call, as they wanted to give me time to think about it and provided me with examples of other commercials and a video from Kevin explaining why I got the call. At the time, for me, this was never going to happen. I had just negotiated a new loan agreement and couldn't possibly afford another $25,000 investment. Hell, I wasn't even sure if I could finish out the year without borrowing more money! I explained to Angie and the boys that we should just forget about it and felt another sense of deflation… Man…F@#k!

The next call that came was from Lisa Vrancken, Executive VP at AsSeenOnTV.pro. I had so many reservations and explained to her that we really couldn't afford this kind of investment. I had done all the research and concluded that this was a legitimate offer, but I was in no position to participate. I expressed to her that I didn't need another fancy commercial, as we had just invested in a new video production for our website and our own television commercial. Again, we were spending money like water, and this was nowhere in the budget! She was so comforting and confident that this would be the right thing for our business, and just to add to the insanity, she invited me to take a spot at their Innovator's Think Tank to be held in Florida. Here I would have an opportunity to meet Kevin in person and pitch our products to a panel of potential buyers and investors. Here was the other catch… It would be an additional $2,000, excluding air fare. What the hell! Now they were asking for more money! I discussed the offer with my wife and kids, and much to my surprise, Angie thought we should do it! She always has been the conservative one of the group, so I struggled with this a bit, as I thought we shouldn't move forward on the offer. We personally had been fortunate in the last few years to also benefit from our retail store's success. We really didn't have the money in our operating budget, but we were sitting pretty well in our personal account. I explained to her that if we moved forward, we would have to take the money out of our personal savings, because we had so many other upcoming expenses. She agreed, and with a knot in my stomach, I informed Lisa that we would move forward with the deal.

The very next day I had buyer's remorse! I called Lisa and she immediately took my call. This was somewhat comforting, as I expected that once we had committed, I would never hear from her again. This all seemed too good to be true, like a scam! Here I was committing to close to $30,000 for the commercial and the trip, as I had decided to take the twins along to the Think Tank. Lisa just had a way of putting my fears to rest; she seemed sincerely concerned with my concerns. She gave me confidence and comfort in telling me that I was doing the right thing, so all that was left to do was to travel down for the Think Tank. Scott, another instrumental partner, also worked with us to delay our second installment for the commercial, as normal protocol was to pay before completion. Since we were going to the Think Tank, they could hold the commercial production to happen while we were in Florida. This gave me some relief for my anxiety, but most of it remained.

So now came the difficult part! We were informed that we would only have three minutes to pitch our product in front of a very influential group of buyers and investors. We really were unsure of how to craft it, since one pitch would work for buyers, but another seemed best for investors. The twins were home doing their internship with us over the summer as we prepared them to return in their full-capacity roles after their last semester of college. We worked long and hard and felt good that we could incorporate the best of both worlds. We rehearsed time after time and were finally ready to make the trip down to Florida. I'm not going to lie, even on the plane ride down, I was thinking, "We're going to land and go to an abandoned warehouse with a note saying... Haha, we tricked you!" This still didn't seem real, but we were about to find out.

Once we arrived, we taxied to the hotel where the Think Tank would be held. It was hard not to be excited, but also not to be nervous. Here was a once in a lifetime opportunity! If we did well, who knows, but if we didn't, all seemed lost. Now, that's a bit of an exaggeration, since we were still running a successful retail store and there was still plenty of potential for our e-commerce business, but this could be a whole different deal! We had a couple of days before the presentation and prepared for the moment. Could this be the very thing we needed to take our company to the next level? I was proud to be sitting with my sons and beginning to build our future together!

The day finally arrived. We woke up early and went down for breakfast. I felt good and confident that we could make something happen and we were ready to give our pitch. This is what I excel at, being an old salesman, so I wasn't worried about a thing! Then the worst possible thing happened... I stared to get nervous and anxious! I had struggled with anxiety as a younger man, but it really wasn't a part of my life anymore. I called my wife before things got started and hoped she could calm me down. She affirmed that I would be fine, but I couldn't shake the anxiety. Here I was in the most important position of my life, and I was starting to second guess myself. I remained distant from the group as I was trying to get my shit together. "Come on, Rod, this is just another pitch." I thought to myself. But it wasn't, it was THE pitch. I finally willed my way into the conference room, but I still couldn't shake the anxiety completely. To make matters worse, we would be the first to give our pitch!

The time had come. We had rehearsed this so many times, but I found myself not being able mentally to get past, "Hi, I'm Rod from Accord Comfort Sleep Systems." It didn't matter, it was go-time. So, the boys and I stepped up and began the pitch. Fortunately, I started strong, but halfway through I lost my place. I looked over at Quincy and he whispered the next line and I finished my portion. The boys finished their part perfectly and we received a strong applause. Once the questions and answers started, I was back in my groove, but still not feeling at my best. Next up we had to meet with the panels individually. This was a quick procedure, so fortunately it didn't afford me time to think about my anxiety. We moved from panel to panel and finally came to Kevin's table. We started to pitch our product again, and Kevin seemed intrigued. We went significantly past our allotted time, and I thought that it was cool that he was so interested in what we were doing. We even prescribed and sent him a mattress that would be good for him and his wife, which they love! Kevin and his wife are sleeping on a CopperRest Gold mattress… How cool is that!

While I was trying to get my shit together pre-conference, the boys were approached by a gentleman named Haresh. He informed them that he was really excited to talk to us about our products and was a partner with Kevin in an overseas venture. I wasn't there for the introduction, but once again the boys represented us well. They were filling me in on the information, and as usual, I was thinking nothing would come of it. I'm normally not such a cynic, but I have learned over the years that some things are simply too good to be true.

The event went by like a whirlwind. We talked to so many people so fast, it was hard to keep up. We made so many contacts, as was promised, and we are currently working with some of the people we met there! This was absolutely the best thing we could have done, even if the commercial wasn't part of it. The next day we proceeded to the spot of the production shoot.

We were invited to the location of our new commercial shoot and we weren't sure what to expect. We went into a gated community via Uber, which was a bit challenging. When we arrived at the house, we met the producer and the homeowner. We were actually shooting a commercial in someone's home, which was nothing like anything I had been involved in before. Any previous television commercials usually involved footage from our retail location or on a green screen! We had also been able to choose two different actors from a talent agency, which I have never been involved with before either. It was like going into a movie production. Even the details of attire were considered. The producer felt that the male actor didn't have what he was looking for, so someone ran to a store and bought the expected attire. This was confirming that all the money spent was well worth the investment! They weren't just shooting a generic sixty-second spot; they were totally committed to an artistic vision.

We were able to hook up with one of our other creative team members who lived in Florida at the time. He had been introduced to me through Bill and did an outstanding job as well. He produced our website videos and made a special trip to be on-site for this commercial. There was nothing to be gained for his time, other than a formal in-person introduction with us and to talk about further creative development. He remains one of our creative talents today.

We left this meeting and the trip with renewed enthusiasm that what we were pursuing was right. We made new business connections that could help our business online, as well as the potential for an international deal if we played our cards right. Even if nothing developed further, we would have a tremendous commercial, a celebrity endorsement, cable network spots in the cities of our choosing, and a lifetime of new friendships with people that were extremely well connected in business! Thank you so much, Lisa, for comforting me and giving me the confidence to attend and commit... My appreciation can never be fully expressed! Thank you to everyone involved, you made this experience an impression of a lifetime!

THE DYNAMIC DUO

One evening as I was getting home late due to all the work involved in the restart, I noticed that Chris and Matt had left me a note on the kitchen table. They were already in bed and asleep as it was a school night. I felt terrible, once again I had barely seen them this day, but this is unfortunately what's required sometimes in order to get things done. I opened the note and started to tear up a bit as they both took the time to draw design sketches of new mattress ideas. My heart was literally swelling with love and pride. They figured that if daddy was working late, so should they. I have to admit that their ideas were pretty good. They had overheard our discussions about creating lower priced products to try to improve sales. One had come up with a plush concept, the other a firm one. Of course, I still have the drawings and carry them with me every day in my briefcase (a real one, not the backgammon case).

A couple of days later, I was looking at their drawings again. I would do this to stimulate my own motivation from their willingness to care, and I started to think about another mattress company that had entered the "bed-in-a-box" business with a two-sided mattress. Maybe I could merge both designs, and come up with our own two-sided mattress, which was unique in the industry at the time. This could also alleviate buyer anxiety, since the customer doesn't get a chance to try the bed before they buy. Here a customer would essentially be buying two beds in one! Since it was two-sided, I would have to change the core design to give equal support, which would in turn lower costs by eliminating our "Accord Comfort Reflex Layer". This would not diminish quality, just a change of cost in the design. We would also be quite different from other competitors, since our construction materials were completely different, unique and quite frankly, better. I started really getting excited about the concept, but of course not about the costs of a new product design and everything else that came with it. We had some discussion with members of our management team, and finally settled on the mattress's new name... DUO. I scheduled a flight to Chicago to meet with the plant owners, this time taking Angie along so I could introduce more of my family to theirs. We came up with the perfect construction combination and awaited a prototype.

I bring this up in the story because this took place before we went to the Think Tank. We were excited about the idea and the tremendous value in the product. This would be our lowest priced mattress, and yet offer two beds in one. It really is exceptional value! When we met with Haresh and some of his partners in Florida, this was one of the products and price points that were talked about. Now this product was in play for potentially huge international distribution, but I hadn't even approved the prototype yet... Man...F@#k! I called Ed at the plant the day after the Think Tank meetings. I had been given broad strokes on what could possibly happen in terms of order volume, and quite frankly they were mind-boggling. I had to be sure that one, we could actually build to that capacity in a timely manner, and two, we could schedule containers for shipment overseas. This was something I had never been involved in before, so here came more learning opportunities! I will admit that I called Ed from a sunny beach in Florida as I had scheduled an extra day off with my sons to celebrate what we had accomplished that week... When in Rome! Ed was instantly excited and like me, couldn't quite believe

117

it was true. We talked about all the details, and he assured me
that from his side, we could get this done. Needless to say, we
did celebrate, but something like this creates many new concerns,
including the possibility of success. Could we handle it, and what
would it look like?

For now, we needed to get the DUO prototype confirmed, as
our next step in the international deal was getting samples to
Haresh. He wanted them as soon as possible because he had
another international trip scheduled. Once we returned home
from Florida, I expected the prototype to be delivered and I could
give my approval on it. I got to work early that day, as I knew our
standard truck had arrived and delivered to our retail location,
but I couldn't find the DUO. Finally, my staff came in, and it was
discovered that it hadn't arrived. I called the plant and somehow it
had been overlooked. Come on! The one time I needed something
right away, and this was our first fumble... Man...F@#k! I
explained that we had to get it out as soon as possible, so we
decided to have the prototype roll packed and sent out UPS in a
box, like we do online. This would be the fastest way for delivery.
Unfortunately, it was a Friday, so the weekend would cause some
delay. It seemed like forever for it to arrive, but it finally made it. I
opened the box, hoping everything was perfect and I could get the
sample order placed the same day to meet our deadline for Haresh.

We opened the box, and... everything was wrong! How could this
be? It was a simple design, and we used a combination of the same
materials of which our other beds are made... Man...F@#k!

I was on the phone for hours making sure we got the design
right, which was difficult when I was not there in person. This
of course created another week-long delay, as we needed to build
a new prototype, then roll pack it and ship it via UPS again. The
second prototype arrived and with much anxiety, we opened the

box. It was perfect! We quickly approved the design and placed the order for the samples. If we got the order built and shipped right away, we could still meet our deadline. We can usually produce a mattress in forty-eight hours, so on day three I called to make sure everything was shipping out, but I was notified that there was a problem. During manufacturing there was a build error and damage, so the DUO would have to be rebuilt. Are you kidding me?! This could be a life-changing contract, and now there was no way we could deliver the samples on time. Haresh was going to think we were completely incompetent! I dreaded making the call, as I was expecting to be told to forget about the whole deal, but I made it anyway. To my surprise, Haresh wasn't even worried about it. It was Monday and he was leaving for India on Thursday and would be gone for a week. So, if we could have the samples delivered when he returned, that would be great. It felt like a fifty-pound weight had been removed from my chest, I could breathe easy again. But he did ask and suggest that I Fed Ex some brochures for him to take along, as he would meet with some of his vendors while he was there. "Sure", I said, the only catch was… we didn't have any! I hung up the phone and immediately called Quincy and Spencer to come to my office. It was about ten o'clock in the morning and I needed to design a brochure from scratch, print one hundred copies and get them shipped out to Fed Ex the same day, so that they could be delivered before Thursday… Man…F@#k!

I had been brought up and had brought my sons up to get to work and bust your ass, so that is what we did. We were only going to feature three of our now six models, so we had to custom design a brochure just for our overseas buyers. We downloaded some software and got to work. It was intense, with a fair amount of yelling back and forth, as creative conflicts were abounding. This normally wouldn't happen, but we didn't have days to create the design - we had less than two hours! I don't think I've mentioned this in the book at all, but our community only has a population of 2,000 people. So, we don't have a printing option or a Fed Ex location. The nearest city with those credentials is seventy-five miles away, so we had to factor drive time into our deadline as well. We were physically sweating once we finished the design, but we had done it! Now the next hurdle, could somebody print one hundred copies while we were on the drive up and get them folded and ready? We called all the major "big box" players and none of them could do it, so I reached out to our usual printing source, and thankfully they obliged. We got there and the brochures were still warm from printing. They looked great, so we headed out to the Fed Ex drop off. I paid what was necessary to get them there on time, and sure enough they did. I received a text confirming they had arrived and Haresh would be taking them along with him on his trip… Man…F@#k!

You would think that the extra time to get Haresh the samples would have been a relief, but somehow without notification, the plant had run out of some of the materials we needed, since the product was still in the prototype stage. This caused another manufacturing delay and pushed the delivery of the samples to the very last day. What should have been such an easy process had turned into a nightmare, but in the end, we still got it done on time! So, where did we go from here?

THE WAITING IS THE HARDEST PART!

Let's set the stage for what was happening to the company internally. Marchand Retail Group, Inc. is our parent corporation. It holds and operates several different businesses, which include Tom's Home Furnishings, our retail store selling furniture, appliances and floorcoverings; Builder Corps, a membership-only program selling furniture, flooring and appliances online direct; Accord Comfort Sleep Systems, manufacturing and selling mattresses online and Amazon and wholesale; Leo R. Rutten Foundation, a non-profit charitable organization; and Marchand Property Holdings, real estate development and leasing. Our retail store is our flagship store and was the only reason we had the opportunity to expand into some of these new ventures. But changes in economy, like oil prices dropping, farm commodity prices dropping, and CP Rail pulling out of the depot in our community and canceling the housing contract, were starting to significantly affect retail sales. Our revenue was still strong, but virtually all profit was being used to subsidize our mattress venture and was even falling short of that. All the setbacks, new product development, website development, carton costs, video production, image file creation, additional inventory that more than doubled in size, had taken its toll. We had just refinanced in the spring and by fall were running out of cash and operating credit. I would have to talk to our bank again… This would be fun… Man…F@#k!

We had been with the same bank for twenty years and had an outstanding relationship with them. Like all small communities, these people weren't just professionals, they were our friends. They were the ones that took a chance on me when I bought out my parents, they were with us during the terrible times, and watched us grow during the good. But thinking like me, the trend wasn't looking good, and I could sense that the next round of financing would be difficult to get. I need to be clear, they were absolutely willing to meet the terms in our proposal, but I just didn't have a good feeling about the future. If any more capital would be needed, would they be there for us?

For many years, another lender had been approaching us to see if they could do business with us in any way. I never really pursued anything, since we were doing really well and didn't have a need to refinance for most of the time… and I'm a pretty loyal guy. I subscribe to "dance with the one who brought ya". So being very happy with where I was, I just never gave them an opportunity. My thinking started to change when I returned home from Florida. I knew my own projections and knew I would run out of cash later in the year. I was going to need to raise capital, and there were really only two ways to do it. One, I could take on investors, or two, I could borrow more money. We had finally bought out any remaining partners a few years before, so investors weren't the way I wanted to go. Lending would have to be the source of capital, but if our international deal went through, what would that success look like? Would we potentially need millions in new credit lines? If so, could our current lender even risk that much exposure, as they were a smaller community bank? If the business was international, would there be a need for currency exchange? And the list went on. I had mentioned these things to our current bank long before we needed the new capital. Some of the answers to the previous questions were, "No", so I thought this might be the time to reach out to the other lender, and see if they not only could, but would do anything for us. I knew Marchand Property Holdings had more equity available in real estate assets than what our balance sheet showed, but this would require an appraisal to find the proper valuation.

I invited the primary contact from the new lender that I was familiar with to visit Quincy, Spencer and me at the store one day, so we could go over a rough draft of what we had in mind. I also wanted him to take a look at the real estate, mattress products, and some of the internal operations, so that he could see that it was actually real... Even I sometimes wondered. The meeting lasted much longer than it should have, but in a good way. He believed, and even promoted, the finance package I proposed. He couldn't have been more excited with what we were doing and thought it was incredible. He was so impressed with what we had built, he just had to be a part of it and couldn't wait to go back and tell the rest of his company. Wow! That went better than expected! After the meeting, the twins and I were reflecting on how things had gone, and everyone agreed that there was an excitement in the air. It was easy to talk finance, since our thought process and theirs seemed perfectly aligned. But most importantly, our cultures seemed to match and they were a very large bank that could offer all the services we would require, if we did have the massive growth and more! Everyone agreed to place an order for an appraisal, for the humble price of $4,000... Man...F@#k!

The bank put us in touch with a group from a larger city in order to get the best perspective appraisal. Once the numbers were generated, it wouldn't take them long to come up with a finance proposal, but until then, there really wasn't much they could say. We still had operating capital available, so there wasn't any immediate hurry. Thank God there wasn't! I had spoken with the gentleman that would be doing the inspection as well as the final appraisal. I think we rescheduled the inspection appointment three times over the span of five weeks. He is a fantastic person, but if I ever needed him to help me in any type of life or death emergency requiring speed, I was done for! I think it took close to eight weeks to finally get the inspection done and we hoped the paperwork would go much faster. It wouldn't... The waiting was the hardest part! This was the very first thing we would need to potentially source new capital, and it took over four months to get the results. This was not the bank's fault; it was completely outside of their control and I know they were probably more frustrated than I was. Once we had the numbers, a proposal was quickly generated, and we accepted. This created a new problem. I would have to inform our existing lender that we had decided to move on after twenty years of great service and friendship. I believed fully that this was the best business decision but felt like I had cheated on a spouse... Another fun upcoming meeting... Man...F@#k!

It's important to mention our lender here. First International Bank was willing to take our newest risk and thought our business had great potential. Let me be clear; our previous bank wasn't looking to shut us down, but I didn't feel that they had the same commitment to our future vision. When we had our discussion with Mark, Jason and Melissa about our current endeavors, we couldn't help but get excited about their belief in our business models. Like any startup company, we still hadn't shown a profit, but they could see the same potential that we saw. Once we moved our business, the excitement carried over to everyone in the organization. You could feel it in every interaction, and everybody seemed to be rooting for us! The bank had a similar start in terms of family as they were a third-generation business just like us. They even brought the president of the bank out from their main headquarters just to see our business for himself! Again, not to knock our previous lender, but we hadn't had this kind of enthusiasm for a long time. It made me feel like I was starting over again for the first time in business, as if it was day one!

We were finally ready and able to move forward with our potential international deal with the new capital in place, but again... the waiting was the hardest part... Man...F@#k!

THAT WAS EASY... NOT!

So, we had new product development in place and the inventory was on the way to Amazon. We now had a two-front issue: getting samples to India for our international customers and stocking our products domestically in Amazon's warehouses. We had agreed to work with our manufacturer on co-branding a mattress of theirs called Harvest. This is an organic mattress and a trending product in the industry, but also required that we commit to more upfront inventory investments and marketing costs. We placed our initial order and waited for everything to be received into Amazon's distribution centers. We had also entered into an agreement with a company we had met in Florida at the Innovator's Think Tank and we were excited to use their expertise in creating these new product listings and marketing. They had a monthly fixed expense, as well as a commission structure in place which I liked, since that would mean they had skin in the game. Still not ready to spend more money, we agreed to our contract with them, hoping that this was the right decision to grow our business on Amazon.

Simultaneously, our international group was requesting that we send samples of our product to India. This is something we had never been involved in before, so once again came the learning process. We had the products built and set up shipping to get them overseas using UPS Air. We had many stumbling blocks, including all types of customs and duty concerns. The shipment would be delayed due to our uncertainty of the international shipping process and this would cause even more stress, as we were expected to get those products by a deadline so we could give a presentation that we subsequently missed... Man...F@#k! I figured that we would again miss our opportunity and blow the deal. Thank God it wasn't a deal-breaker, but it would cause delay in our partnership development. What next?

In the meantime, our products were starting to arrive at Amazon. We were excited about the new product and sales opportunities and we were excited about what the new company we had hired could do for us. It was so refreshing working with professionals that knew what needed to be done and more specifically, I didn't have to do it! We had already seen sales growth from the moment we hired them, so we couldn't wait to get these new products launched. Finally, everything was received, and we were ready to go live with them on Amazon. We had now almost tripled our inventory investment, so even with the new capital in place, we would start to tax our operating lines if this wasn't successful. We started to launch our new online marketing campaign, and sure enough we sold our first DUO. Awesome! Only, I got a call from our new Amazon account manager to say that something was reset in our listing pricing structure and we sold the mattress for $12.99! This is an $849 retail product and he asked me if we should cancel the order... Man...F@#k! I didn't want to start our new product launch with a potentially negative customer review, so I instructed him that we would let the sale process. I reached out to the buyer, explaining that clearly you couldn't buy a queen size mattress for $13, but would allow the transaction to proceed, simply asking that if he liked the product, he would give us a good review. I saw a couple of weeks later that we did receive a glowing review, as he did indeed love his new mattress. At the end of the review, he made a comment that, "He would have gladly paid two or even three times the price of this mattress!" I found a lot of humor in this, since only he and I knew what he had paid... Man...F@#k! We worked out the bugs and were excited about the future of our new offerings.

After nearly three weeks of delay, our product samples finally made it to India. Of course, by the time we paid the freight to get them there, the shipping cost was actually more than the value of the products... Man...F@#k! But you have to do what is necessary to succeed. This created another concern, as we were asked what it would cost to ship our mattresses overseas by container - another completely unknown venture we had never worked with. Haresh and his team already had a shipping broker in place, but they were not yet doing business in our category, so nobody knew for sure what the cost would be. I had zero experience in international shipping and from the recent sample ordeal, I was feeling unsure!

Now that the samples had arrived, things were progressing nicely and it seemed that we could work out a deal, but this would be the next hurdle in our business relationship. I had traveled to attend a fundraising event in which my niece was participating and received a very positive phone call from Haresh and his team that we would be making our way to India to give a presentation to potential buyers at a time still to be determined. I was feeling very excited and mentioned to the group at the event that things were looking quite promising. As I mentioned this to my niece, I was very surprised to learn that she specialized in international logistics for her employer. What the hell, how did I not know this?! I was impressed at all the knowledge she had, even though the company she was working for wasn't specifically in our industry. Although I had had some cocktails, I forewarned her that I would be reaching out for help. The following Monday, I called and explained what we were doing and where we were going with our new venture. She immediately took the lead and negotiated the terms of our shipping contract and much to our surprise, she negotiated a great rate and contract! What a small world and once again, I couldn't help but see providence at work! I also mentioned that if things were going to happen, maybe she would have to come on board and work with our company... I love family business!

Like everything in life, you live, and you learn! That was easy... not! But here we were, on the brink of a life-changing opportunity and all the pieces of the puzzle were starting to fall in place! In a good way... Man...F@#k!

Like everything in life, there is no magic wand. If you really want to succeed at anything - life or business - you must work hard. Another well-known fact is that you better be prepared to make adjustments and even start from scratch if necessary. After all the latest hurdles and learning curves, things were far from finished. We continued to wait for confirmation on the travel details to India. Some new concerns developed in terms of cost/retail price and how our products would market to the wholesale/retail customer. We had tremendous feedback about the design and comfort of the samples that were sent, both from retailers and customers. However, as should have been expected, the products that are built and sold in India are different in terms of size and price. So, as we awaited news from abroad on how to proceed, we began to realize the difficulty of doing business across the globe. We were eleven hours apart, so correspondence became difficult. Every email was a day from sending to reply. Days quickly turned to weeks, and then to months. Although we were making strides in terms of business every day, it seemed like the wind was being knocked out of our sails and the process was such a grind. Not that doing business on an international scale was the only opportunity, but it was something that could completely change the immediate dynamic of our business, so it was difficult not to be excited about what that could mean for our future and what we could do as a company for the world!

If there was any potential providence in the coming delays, is would be that Quincy and Spencer were set to graduate from the Carlson School of Management, University of Minnesota during the third week of December. Although they were finishing their last year in college, they still remained active in the decision making of this new venture. As I said before, they might have made a bigger impact than I did when we first met the parties involved. Don't let me fool you, not having them physically present to help with development and design still put a tremendous burden on me in terms of trying to work out these details with the communication delays and after hour work requirements. So, it goes without saying that I couldn't wait for them to return home and take on their full-time responsibilities within the company.

In the meantime, we quickly discovered that we had joint venture opportunities in India. We had been working closely with Charak, a partner of Haresh running an up and coming business venture in India. I shouldn't need to remind you that India has over 1.3 billion people, making this retail market very substantial. Everyone knew that we had great mattress products, focused on comfort and health, but it became clear that we would have to come up with new designs to specifically target the consumer in India. Oh, this story was becoming too familiar! This meant new brand names, construction design, image files, etc... Which just meant more time and money... Just when I thought it was safe to get back into the water... Man...F@#k!

My son Spencer graduated with two degrees - one in supply chain management so his cap stone classes included international shipping. This would now become handy because he would be able to talk to Caroline, previously handling all of our overseas shipping contracts. After some further discussion, Caroline was unable to jump on board full-time with our organization. Again, providence seemed to be at work, as I thought we would need to secure all the shipping details before the twins graduated, but now we had time to make the transition. We had discussed joint venture retail options with Charak, which included selling on Amazon India and starting a D2C website business. So along with designing new products, we would now look at new Amazon listings, image files, content and another website! Am I in the movie Ground Hog Day?... Man...F@#k!

SWEET HOME CHICAGO

Off we go, into the wild blue yonder... back to Chicago. I had been delaying another trip to design the new products since it would make the most sense to fly from Chicago to India for our upcoming presentation. I hadn't talked to Haresh in a few weeks, so I waited to hear about travel dates, as he himself had been traveling abroad. When we did get together on a call, I was informed that until we develop the new products and submit our new price structure, there would be no need to schedule the trip. That would have been useful three weeks ago! Now I would need to scurry out the plant and come up with two more designs.

Ed and his family had been absolutely wonderful to work with. As I mentioned earlier, I love the fact that they are family-owned and have such a personal touch, perfectly in line with our company! Ed and his team have been critical in making all the adjustments required for new product design and had provided me with critical knowledge in terms of manufacturing and wholesale advice. He was slowly becoming a new mentor and partner! It is so important to seek guidance from someone you know and trust who has a commitment to the same ideas and strategy that you have. I feel our relationship has grown into so much more than simply business partners - we have become friends, confiding in each other in business and in life. I can't wait for our families to meet each other!

I had intended on taking the twins along, but the trip would have to be scheduled during finals week. Another hurdle arose - we had planned a trip to Green Bay to watch the Packers play the Bears as a Christmas gift to our four sons. This would be Christopher and Matthew's first ever game, so I didn't want to cancel. I decided to watch the game on Sunday, then fly from Green Bay to Chicago on Monday, work a couple of days and head back home on Wednesday... Man...F@#k! We are huge Green Bay Packer fans and our partners in Chicago are obviously Bear's fans. The game resulted in a Packer victory. Would they even let me into the plant? Just kidding!

Leading up to this trip I only had a couple of weeks to prepare. Again, when you communicate with partners overseas, things don't develop quickly. I already had some design concepts in mind, so I had a head start on the logo design and color. What I needed from them was overall thickness specifications and wholesale price points. When I finally received the email I had been waiting for, my heart sank! The entry level price they wanted to meet would be nearly impossible to hit. Especially since we would be exporting from the USA to India, something that was appealing to the consumer in India. I also knew that I wouldn't consider compromising on manufacturing quality and construction, so I felt pretty sure we had hit the end of the road. After all this investment, both in money and time, would nothing come of it? Man...F@#k!

If you haven't figured it out yet, I'm a "Type A" personality. I had opened the email at about 2:00 am, as I had my phone next to me on my nightstand and heard the email alert. I don't recommend this policy to anyone, but that is how I roll. I also don't recommend checking your email at 2:00 am, as you will surely be up for the day. Another sleepless night as I awaited a response to my latest email explaining our inability to drive manufacturing costs that low. I did get a reply the same morning and much to my relief,

Charak also agreed to my points. There were some suggested prices compared to other companies in India, but he agreed that we wouldn't want to lose our uniqueness of products and recognized the value of being "Made in the USA" to help demand higher retail prices. This was a huge relief. We had quoted some actual best wholesale prices before my trip, just to make sure there would be need for the trip. Everyone agreed that we were on the right path, so off I went... sweet home Chicago!

While all of this was going on, I had been in contact with another potential venture opportunity. I was introduced to Matt by Bill - the guy who had helped us with some web design. Matt is a successful inventor and entrepreneur. He invented an impact gel technology that could be used in many different product categories, one of them being mattress products. We had a few different phone conversations and emails and felt like the next thing to do was meet. Since we would have to discuss how his gel could be incorporated into our manufacturing process, I thought it best to meet with him in Chicago, and spend a day talking about business opportunities. As soon as we met, we hit it off right away! He was full of energy and had the exact same company values as us. He had made many different celebrity contacts from previous product launches and had some upcoming meetings that could help us launch on a massive scale both nationally and internationally. Once again, I was unbelievably excited about what opportunities could arise, I was killing multiple birds with one stone, but I needed to focus on one thing at a time... Man...F@#k!

As soon as I finished my meeting with Matt, it was off to the design room to finish two new products. One would be a 6" mattress called Bliss, and the second would be a modified 7" CopperRest mattress called Jade. We would keep the DUO in the India line up, so finally we would have our three mattress line up. The design meeting was intense, but in the end, we came up with great new products and a price matrix to satisfy the market. I called my sons during finals week and had them work with me late into the night so that we could create a wholesale spreadsheet, detailing all the shipping, taxes and duties on these new mattresses. I absolutely wanted to get this information emailed to Charak that night, so he would see it first thing in the morning.

I woke up at 4:00 am, not for any reason other than to check my email. There in my inbox was a reply from Charak. I almost didn't want to open it! What if the prices didn't work? I was to leave around lunch time to return home, so I really wouldn't have time to go back to the drawing board. I click on the email and thankfully he thought the prices looked great! Well done team! I was now fully awake and began to pack up my hotel room for the flight home. Remember, we still ran a pretty big retail store and I had plenty of work to complete on that front. Plus, the upcoming week was Christmas, Quincy and Spencer were moving back home for good as college graduates, I had a company Christmas party scheduled for the next weekend, including a Think Tank of my own for my employees to prepare for, and now another email from Charak wanting new brochures for the new mattress line up by next Monday... Just living the dream... Man...F@#k!

RETURN OF THE JEDI

So, as I mentioned, the boys graduated college and moved back home. Now it was time to get to work! We had a great Christmas party, but as I mentioned, I had a Think Tank meeting before the party started to try and get new ideas and policy implementation for our future. I was focused on appointing new department heads and trying to implement how Quincy and Spencer would work within the company. This would be a challenge, since I experienced some of the same struggles I knew that they would experience being young and taking on management responsibilities like I did when I rejoined the company back in my earlier days. They had always been well respected. Like me, they had grown in the business from working on the labor side as teenagers. They worked the warehouses and they worked on the flooring installation team, so all of our employees knew them very well. They were brought up to work hard and always had a great attitude regarding work, so it wasn't hard to incorporate them into the day to day operations.

I appointed Quincy in the role of flooring department manager and COO of the company. Spencer was appointed department head of all our e-commerce ventures and CFO of the company. We had a great meeting and even included a classmate of theirs that would take charge of our digital graphic design and marketing responsibilities. All seemed to be right with the world. The Think Tank meeting went very well, and we gleaned many new great ideas, some which are already implemented today. We transitioned into the party and celebrated what the future would hold and really picked up on the excitement and opportunities of the future. It was a very exciting party, and everyone was focused on making our company a better business. Even one of the employees coined the phrase "Our vision for the future is 2020!" Very clever I thought, although that was going to change... We'll get to that in the next chapter!

It wasn't all rainbows and roses. There would be some pushback from older employees wondering why they might have been passed over in terms of promotion to department heads, something I did anticipate with the boys being younger and fresh out of college. Also, although Quincy and Spencer were very intelligent, they still had to make use of their college experience and finally incorporate it into industry knowledge. We made the shifts in policy but had many setbacks in making sure the proper executions were met. Like any family business, this put stress on our relationships, and I found myself coaching them in terms of their new responsibilities. I love my sons, but we still needed to run a company and the time to execute was now!

When we were first preparing for our meeting in Florida with the AsSeenOnTv and Innovators Think Tank with Kevin Harrington, we crafted our pitch to include not only what made our mattress products different, but we also wanted to pitch investment opportunities to start a domestic wholesale distribution network. We saw how the "bed-in-a-box" industry was failing in delivering quality products and was having a high return rate. We were extremely proud of the fact that our return rate was less than one percent, when most of our major competitors were around thirty percent! We had the vision of setting up other domestic retailers across the country. That way customers had the ability to try our products at a local brick and mortar store, then either take our mattress home, order online, or have a white glove delivery option. Although we didn't have immediate success during our pitch, we still didn't lose sight of developing this business model.

We were making great strides with our international partnership and continued to be in contact with our future partners in India. All the pieces were in place with Charak and Haresh. Our business model was starting to shape up and our trip was finally going to happen. While all this was developing, I got a call from Ed, our manufacturing partner from Chicago. He saw the opportunity we were presenting and mentioned that he could get us space in a regional market in the upper Midwest to show our products on the wholesale level. Needless to say, we were very excited and immediately committed to the market. Once again, this would cost our company money in terms of the floor space and samples required to show our mattress. It didn't matter, this was the opportunity we needed to finally launch our domestic wholesale business!

Spencer, Quincy and I put together all our marketing materials and began to put all the necessary pieces in place. This was another business expense we didn't have the money for and another unknown process of our business. We had been in retail all our lives - How could we convince other retailers to do business with us wholesale? What set us apart and what profit opportunities did we present? All we knew was that we made great products and now they could be seen in terms of build and feel.

In the meantime, we continued to move forward with our international partners and the future looked bright. We were now having video conferences and we were discussing legal partnerships in forming a new company in India. This even included potentially manufacturing overseas and other retail outlets including the UAE. Even though all of this was taking place, we still had to prepare for our upcoming market and seemed ready to go. Spencer would be the one to accompany me for this trip and Quincy would stay behind managing the day-to-day of our retail business. Though they were still learning their roles in the company, Angie and our entire staff were willing to step up to the plate and make sure that things would run smoothly while we continued these new ventures. Spencer had also been in contact with one of the largest shipping brokers/companies in the world, CH Robinson, and conveniently scheduled a meeting with our regional rep on the way to our market. Business was still very busy in our retail business, and we trusted that everyone would be remarkable and do their jobs. We ventured out on a Tuesday afternoon and had an evening meeting with our rep regarding how we could continue to negotiate the best shipping terms, both internationally and domestically. This couldn't have come at a better time... Was this providence?

We arrived at the halfway point to our market to have a meeting with our CH Robison representative. This seemed very efficient to me and I didn't know what to expect. I would have preferred to drive further so we could get set up earlier, but I felt the meeting was important. We met up for drinks and started our conversation about what they could do for us. Spencer being a supply chain graduate, immediately started to have an intelligent conversation about what we needed, both in terms of international and domestic shipping requirements and I immediately started to feel relieved! This was what I had waited for, letting go of some of the business responsibilities, especially in the scope of things in which I was unfamiliar. I listened to the guys talk and felt comfortable letting them work out the details. I was also extremely proud to watch my son take command and control of the meeting. I even left the meeting for a while as I mentioned that I really didn't want to know the details - that's what I had Spencer for! I had checked in with Quincy and our retail store and everything else were going great... Awesome!

Our meeting was very productive and made all of our new ventures appear as if they were going to go smoothly, giving us confidence in the upcoming market. The next morning, we got up early so we could get to the market location due to the fact that we would have to set up our display area and get checked in to something we had never been a part of before. We were loading up the car to head for the road when suddenly Spencer remarked, "Shit!" I was loading up my briefcase and luggage when I asked him what was the matter? He expressed that he was missing his laptop, which had our digital and video presentation for the market on it. We rummaged through the car, then quickly discovered that he had forgotten it in his office at home... Man...F@#k! I was disappointed, but we could figure out another way to upload the material to my computer and things would be fine. I took a moment to express how being thorough is critically important and next time we couldn't have a letdown like this. Ironically, when I was loading my gear, I had set a folder that had all our POP materials needed for the market on top of the car next to me, and when he exclaimed that he was missing his laptop, I began searching the car. Once we determined that he had forgotten it, I got in the car frustrated and running short of time and left my folder on the car next to us in the parking lot! We wouldn't discover this until we arrived at the market location... Man...F@#k!

We finally arrived at the market around noon and scoped out our presentation space. None of our products were set up and we needed to recover all the lost materials. During the trip, we received an email from Haresh wanting to set up a video call that same afternoon. No way would we not make that meeting, so we ran like crazy to multi-task! We proceeded to get our display set up and still make it to our hotel room for the call. It couldn't have gone better. We were informed that we needed some documentation to setup our international partnership and that our trip would finally be scheduled very soon. Awesome! We still needed our

POP materials and went to the hotel business center to print what was missing. As usual, this was more difficult to accomplish, but eventually we did it. Since the market only started at 5:00 pm that night, we scrambled to get things ready..

The first night was flat... It is very difficult to get other retailers who don't know our brand to even visit us. We did our very best but were discouraged about the lack of prospects. The next day was much better and the overall market gave us about seven very good prospects, three of which were willing to place our mattress brand in their stores! Overall, this was a great success and trip. Even though we had spent hours working on our feet all day, here we were, finally getting our mattress company to the trajectory we had envisioned. In a high five perspective... Man...F@#k! I'm thankful for the return of the Jedi.

COVID 19 – THE MAN...F@#K! HEARD AROUND THE WORLD!

Spencer and I were heading home after the market feeling pretty confident in what we had achieved. Our retail operations were flourishing and our e-commerce business had been growing as expected. What could possibly stop us now? We had been hearing news about a virus that was taking place in China, but really didn't see what impact this could have on us. We would get back to work and continue to build our dreams and empire... All was well with the world.

Once we returned home however, it didn't take long to learn about the Corona Virus. At first it seemed to be an isolated issue that wouldn't affect our business. That would change shortly, as it became clear that it was spreading across the globe and becoming a potential pandemic! We soon got reports that our partners in India were majorly affected by the virus and that the country had been put on lockdown. It also didn't take long to find out that the spread of the virus had reached the USA. Obviously, this impacted our international plans and everything we had been working on up to this point was on hold... Man...F@#k! It also affected our domestic plans as particular states started to shut down retail operations. Our new wholesale customers weren't ready at this time to commit to new products, as many of them were ordered to shut their business operations down. This included our Amazon and e-commerce business. Suddenly, Amazon was only shipping essential medical supplies and other related products. The state that we are based has a low population, so we didn't see the immediate effect on our business right away. However, we soon discovered that this would affect everyone in the human race!

As government started to dictate which services were essential and non-essential, even our state was affected. I felt bad for the non-essential businesses that were forced to shut down. This also had a trickle-down effect, as many of our retail customers had to put projects on hold and the future looked very uncertain. As a retail business, we offer services that include flooring installation, furniture and appliance delivery and installation, and even in-home appliance service repair. Once we realized the magnitude of the situation, though we were considered by our state government "essential" and could stay open, we elected voluntarily to shut down our in-home services to quarantine our staff to ensure that they were healthy and safe. We also took the time to lock our retail store and take customers on an appointment basis only, considering the health and safety of our staff and customers.

If there is one funny observation in all of this, it is that once we put our retail location on a two-week lock down, we actually had a substantial increase in business! I had given all of our staff the next two weeks off, and as is the usual benefit of running your own business, Quincy, Spencer, Angie and I went in everyday to serve our scheduled appointments. I remember laughing with them, stating that maybe I really hadn't been running the business correctly prior… Apparently locking the doors is the way to go! I don't at all intend to make light of the pandemic, but we still need to laugh a little and enjoy the blessings we have in life!

I have never been a part of something so significant and I hoped that we could learn how to come out of a situation like this stronger and better than we were before. Everything we had been working towards came to a complete standstill! We continued to work with our customers on all fronts, as we negotiated our business the best we could.

I was confident that as a society we would become stronger due to the pandemic. We were definitely all in it together and I hoped that we would finally break down the barriers of race, creed, and country! I had the privilege of hearing an astronaut speak at one of my recent conferences and he mentioned that when he was able to see the Earth from such a distance in space, he noticed no borders or distinctions... just one planet and one human race. God bless everyone, that is the right perspective!

SCHADENFREUDE!

This is a term I learned in a philosophy class I took some years back. It basically defines the unfortunate human desire to be disappointed when someone else experiences success and to be happy when that same person fails. My very first experience with this was with my father. As I mentioned earlier, when my dad decided to leave the Navy to start his own business, my parents didn't have much. We moved into low-income housing because they were starting a company from nothing. I am very proud to say that they bought their first home in less than two years from the opening of the store! It took many more years to achieve some measure of financial success, but finally my dad was able to buy his first brand new fishing boat. We were very excited to try it out. After his purchase, we were filling up the boat with gas to go on the very first launch. As we were at the gas station, another person from our community shouted out to us, "Must be nice, maybe I should open a furniture store!" I felt bad for my dad, as he never flaunted anything and is probably the most frugal person that I know, but I loved his response as he replied, "It is pretty nice!" I was proud of what my family had achieved but I got my first lesson in, "We're happy that you are having success, as long as you are not more successful than us!"

It is unfortunate that this is a reality of business and entrepreneurship, but you will get pushback as your business grows and success starts to follow. Over the years, we have had great support from customers that have been doing business with us since our company's inception in 1980. This is so awesome, as you build relationships and truly become friends with your customers in a small town. However, unfortunately you can experience a negative effect as jealousy can soon creep in.

Remember the ex-employ formerly known as the "Energy Vampire" in previous chapters? That same person was overheard at a Fourth of July picnic exclaiming that our company would probably go bankrupt due to all the business he was taking away from us. As most small towns go, we heard this rumor from a credible source, and I felt bad that there would even be people that would listen to such nonsense! We have given back over $300,000 to local schools, programmes and other charitable donations in our community for the last 40 years, so why would anyone be hoping for our failure? Obviously, that person was still not over the fact that we let him go, but that is the reality of human nature... I wish it wasn't so! Even when I let him go, it was actually a gesture of goodwill. See, my action wasn't out of some malicious intent or power trip, I knew in order for him to grow and achieve his personal goals, it couldn't be with our company. Sometimes people just aren't a good fit together, especially when you don't have your personal values aligned with the company's values. Each member of staff either adds value or extracts it. The ideal target is to find a company's purpose and then to live it both personally and professionally! It's disappointing how we lose understanding of expressions and language, such as when something goes wrong and people say, "I didn't do it on purpose!" That is precisely the problem, you didn't "do it on purpose..." See, that's the goal - find your purpose in life and start doing it!

As our retail business expanded, we started to notice a disturbing trend that it was more and more difficult to retain local support.

Our commercial flooring business was growing, but it required us to have to go further away in our trade area. I found it ironic that customers who didn't even know us were giving us tremendous large-scale opportunities based on our ability and competitiveness, yet we would struggle to retain our local friends and neighbors as customers. We have done business hundreds of miles from our original location, and I am proud of the fact that our staff continues to execute and be remarkable! We have also sold thousands of products to customers all over the USA in our e-commerce ventures and consider them equally important, as every customer, big or small, matters to us!

I have had many of my own schadenfreude experiences in terms of personal gain. We have a lake house and purchased a new pontoon that I made sure was never brought into our hometown with the concern for what others might say. We have been careful about buying new cars with the concern for what others might say. All of this seems crazy and unjustified when you realize what risk and hard work is required to own and operate your own business. Our local retail store requires us to sell $100,000 per month just to break even! That doesn't even include our mattress company and e-commerce ventures we sell nationally and, potentially, globally. Considering that we start every month at zero, that is a pretty large nut to crack! We have so many employees and their families depend on us. It doesn't matter what the monthly sales are, they still rely on us. Not to mention the huge investment we have in our local community. We have over 20,000 square feet of real estate and such a huge investment in inventory.

More importantly than financial investment, is the willingness to give back time. I have served on multiple boards, volunteered for youth programs, community projects and I teach religious education for both teens and adults. It's not uncommon to put in fifty to sixty-hour work weeks, though most people will only remark about how I left a little early on a Friday. Even as I write this book, I consider what people might say: "Who does he think he is to write a book?" But you know what, I don't care, and you shouldn't either! I have had many spiritual directors in past years, but I was given a quote that I still have posted on my credenza to look at everyday while I work. It is from Nelson Mandela's inaugural speech in 1994 and it reads, "Our deepest fear is not that we are inadequate; our deepest fear is that we are powerful beyond measure. It is our light, not our darkness that most frightens us. We ask ourselves, Who am I to be brilliant, gorgeous, talented and fabulous? You are a child of God. Your playing small doesn't save the world. There's nothing enlightened about shrinking so that other people won't feel insecure around you. We were born to make manifest the glory of God that is within you. It's not just in some of us it's in EVERYONE. As we let our own light shine, we unconsciously give other people permission to do the same. As we are liberated from our own fear our presence automatically liberates others." I think this sums up everything perfectly! We must interrupt these cycles of bitterness, gossip and hatred, and help one another shine!

This has been the most major shift in my leadership philosophy. I no longer look at what is expected of me in terms of my starting point, my dreams and passions, and what others have to say. I have learned so much from everyone involved in my life and business over the years. I think that might be the most important part of the process. My dad had a very micromanagement style and philosophy, which gave him control over every aspect of the business but restricted his ability to grow. I evolved in my understanding that the smartest person in the room is "all of us!" I have given everyone in the company the ability to become the best versions of themselves if they choose to, and let them become part of the overall management strategy. I have also learned to constantly research and glean information from anyone I am in contact with, always growing from other's experiences. One of the most important implementations I started years ago was setting personal and professional goals and posting them on a white board directly on the opposite wall facing my desk. This way, every time I glance up, I must face them and see how I'm progressing. I have even implemented this policy in our January staff meeting, where I have the group write down three yearly goals - two personal and one professional - which I report to them at their year-end review. Holding yourself accountable and reminding yourself what you intend to do is paramount to achievement!

One last exercise I have used for years is having a great sounding board discussion with myself. Sometimes, I think I am my best mentor and friend! I think about the old classic movie *What About Bob,* where the main character, Bob, seeking psychological care, recites this poem "Roses are red, violets are blue, I'm a schizophrenic and so am I!" I'm only poking fun at myself, not the disorder, as I have had some of the most intense conversations about life and business with simply just myself! I know there are many more of you out there! I encourage you to continue to pursue whatever goals and dreams you have, regardless of fear and restrictions! Trust your instincts and believe in yourself... Together we can change the world!

GOING FROM "REALLY GOOD" TO "GREAT"

I love to read, though you might think I never have time! I think it's important to get as many different perspectives on business as possible, especially from those who have had failures as well as success. If I have found the most consistent theme among men and women who have experienced success, it is that they have always had multiple failures along the way. This changes the mindset of "win or lose" to "win or learn." A recent book I read entitled *Good to Great* sparked one of the newest cultural shifts in my company. I felt that this was exactly where we were, or actually, I would have ranked us as "really good," but somehow, we still couldn't cross the final hurdle to "great." The challenge is tough for any team. If I were to rank us in terms of performance percentage, I would say we run at around ninety-six percent. If you were a student, you wouldn't sneeze at that metric! But I believe we could achieve the goal of operating at one hundred percent of our capacity. Now remember, I'm not talking about being perfect, but being excellent. There is a tremendous difference. I have been driving a culture of personal/professional excellence by being remarkable every day. This doesn't mean life won't happen, remember the title of this book is Man...F@#k! It means that if you approach everything you do with the mindset of giving the best of your ability, you will be excellent and remarkable. Success breeds success and has a ripple effect throughout the whole company.

This is how I want to conclude this book. I don't have any final answers about the future of our company ventures, and as Nike says, "There is no finish line!" With everything happening in the world, it is unsure how the future of business will conclude. I do have all the pieces in place to form our new international partnership and we have domestic wholesale opportunities right around the corner. We have every intention of growing our retail business and venturing into other market opportunities as well. I don't measure our business success on income and balance sheet statements only. Although extremely important, I believe that financial success becomes the natural trailing order of a company who is focused on their why or purpose.

We have had several exciting updates and continue to realign the company with the return of the twins to our management team full-time. We have promoted other team members in order to appoint specific division managers. This should allow me more free time to focus on our mattress wholesale international and domestic growth, while maintaining the ability to actively be involved in our retail operation. We have actively called upon every employee to step up and manage their specific service teams and I really believe that we will get from "really good" to "great" by working together. I think this will become paramount based on what we have gone through as a people and encourage everyone to work together collectively, not only as my company, but as humanity!

My main purpose for writing this book is to connect with any of you who are out busting your ass every day! Whether it's managing a company, owning your company or trying to start up a new company, it's important to know that you're not alone in terms of failures and growing pains. Most importantly, I wanted to share with you that dedication, vision, dreams and goals are achievable if you believe and get to work. If you find yourself thinking, "That's not possible for me" or, "Who am I to think I could dream so big?" then you must change your way of thinking! I can't stress enough the power of positive thought and surrounding yourself with positive people who inspire and motivate you. If there is one thing I have finally learned in life it's this: "The ONLY thing you can control in life is yourself." Life is going to happen... there will be great days and bad days. How you react and what you learn from them is up to you. How you conduct yourself will translate to the people you lead, so lead by example. Be sure to set goals and take action on achieving those goals in all areas of life - both personal and professional. It's important to dream big, but a goal without a plan is simply just a dream. You need to make it a reality! Stop settling for anything less than the best version of yourself, then go out and help others shine, too! Be sure to make the most of your time. We all have the same twenty-four hours in a day, so use them wisely. Focus on the good in life, there really is so much out there, and don't bitch so much. Remember it's alright to treat yourself and enjoy all the great things in your life. Don't wait, make today the first day of your new commitment and become the most positive person you know! Once you get started, make sure you keep your momentum and don't over-complicate things. Remember, most of the stuff we worry about in the future never happens, they're just stories we make up in our heads. Try to focus on one thing at a time, so you can give the action item your fullest attention and develop the best strategy.

Now I'm not painting the world full of unicorns and rainbows, remember the title of the book is Man...F@#k! There is so much in life that is outside of your control. So again, don't try to control it... you can't! Focus on your goals, your attitude, your thoughts and your actions... This is truly what you control. Remember our mission statement: "In every encounter and every interaction, we must leave the world a better place than we found it. Be remarkable today!" The key is discipline...this sets the boundaries for life, allowing us to move freely and at full speed, even in all our imperfections, making us FULLY ALIVE! If we all start looking and acting through the lenses of love, together we can change the world. Now simply go out and make it happen.

BE REMARKABLE TODAY

ACKNOWLEDGEMENTS

I would like to acknowledge the following people who have inspired me along the way to write this book:

Firstly, to my parents for giving me life and the opportunity to build a company from nothing. From humble beginnings to what we have today. Without their support and confidence, I could have achieved nothing!

My wife and children who have supported me in all my endeavors. Even when things looked tough and like there was no hope, they always were there for me to keep pushing me forward and provided me unconditional love.

All of my business associates that I have worked with throughout the years - Ron Dunn, Ed Ciolkosz, Bill Napier, Jack Sears and so many others. Always making it seem that my dreams were right around the corner!

All our friends and customers that never lost site of the tremendous work that we were doing in our community in terms of expansion and growth, truly providing the fuel to continue to strive for great things!

Our employees and staff who made all of this possible with their dedication and commitment to being remarkable and believing in our culture. They are the engine that makes it work!

Haresh Mentha for taking a chance on a start up like ours and giving us the opportunity to do something great for the world!

Kevin Harrington for the inspiration to finally complete the book and all the relationships that he has provided!

Finally, God, for all the guidance, wisdom and inspiration given to me and the confidence to become the man I was intended to be!

ABOUT THE AUTHOR

Rod F. Marchand is the president and CEO of Marchand Retail Group, Inc. operating multiple businesses including retail, wholesale, and manufacturing. As a second generation, family-owned business operation, he is excited to welcome his sons into the transition of a third-generation ownership group. Rod is a proud husband and father of seven children and currently three grandchildren, dedicated to inspiring other entrepreneurs to seek out achieving their dreams and goals!

Starting with just a simple education and proudly admitting a graduate from the school of hard knocks, he has taken a small retail business to the hopes and aspirations of becoming an international business and global brand. His main goal in life is to promote individuals to follow their dreams, work hard and focus on becoming the best versions of themselves. Nothing proves more rewarding than to see others succeed and bring out the best in humanity.

If you wish to learn more about his business journey or how to find help in getting the most out of your personal or professional goals, feel free to contact him at rodfmarchand@hotmail.com.

CPSIA information can be obtained
at www.ICGtesting.com
Printed in the USA
LVHW040928280820
664155LV00005B/630